Plain Song

CLIFF ASHBY

Plain Song

Collected Poems 1960-1985

First published in Great Britain 1985 by
Carcanet Press Ltd
208-212 Corn Exchange Buildings
Manchester M4 3BQ

Some of these poems first appeared in the *Spectator*,
to whose editor thanks are due.

The publisher acknowledges the financial assistance of
the Arts Council of Great Britain

British Library Cataloguing in Publication Data

Ashby, Cliff
Plain song.
I. Title
821'.914   PR6051.S45

ISBN 0-85635-562-3

Typeset by Bryan Williamson, Swinton, Berwickshire
Printed in England by Short Run Press, Exeter

CONTENTS

Agony in the Garden

She sat by the window
Her face expressionless,
Fingers moving in slow
Surrender at her dress.

Hot summer lay around
And the pregnable rose
Lifts her head from the ground
For the passionate nose.

In a bush, a thrush sings
Evangelical lays;
His mate, drooping her wings
Is consumed by a phrase.

Alone with her distress
And her heart all aflame,
She's unable to bless
And unwilling to blame.

All her whites shall be grey
And her window panes black
All her teeth shall decay
And her skin shall grow slack.

And a sword pierce her gut
Cleave her flesh to the bone
And the devil shall cut
Out her heart for his own.

For Grandma

In the twilight of her time,
When every day was dumb
And what was said was not received,
Letters spoke of "sickness, the crime
Of growing old, head grown numb,
The cold, boredom unrelieved."

We wrote spasmodically,
Duty bound. "Children are well,
Don't get round to writing much, we
Apologise." Did we tell
You of the racked brain and mind
To find words cursory but kind?

No more will rain spoil your day
With spite, nor wind waken you
At night, with its malicious play.
The word became flesh and grew,
Assumed a malignant form,
Kept your faded spirits warm.

Under the Hammer

The reduced nanny, smell of talcum powder
Still in her nose, opened her napkin soft heart.
The mistress liked things nice. The breakfast tray
Laid so, her bath regular as milking time,
The *Telegraph* to graze upon at ten.
Life the same, yesterday, today, forever.
The horrors of war had proved most bleak,
Cat food had been so difficult to get.
Society evacuating its fecal
Strata into her house, had caused acute
Discomfort to the family doctor.
Life and the evening sky seemed set for sunshine.

But came the fat, bullying son-in-law,
Given to public anger, impervious
To the subtle snub and well bred silences.
Took first the favourite daughter, then the farm,
Crumbled her comfort in his hammer mill,
Offered the solicitor violence.
Now she stumbles in a haze of spirit,
With two well-hung dogs, the neutral common.

Happy New Year

Let us assess the first month of the year,
One heavy cold, a Brahms occasioned tear,
Five slips expressing editors' regrets,
Eight games of snooker, half a dozen bets,
Two visits from the curate who with skill
Unwittingly disseminates ill-will.
Two eyes to watch my daughters grow and bless,
One wild mad tongue to lash them to distress,
A sudden sigh for people in the street,
Rude thoughts about the butcher and his meat.
We don't know where we go but on we plod,
Pursued by lust and shame and nudged by God.
It seems this bright New Year bids fair to be
Full of fertility, but not for me.

Culture

We talked; it seemed my northern accent hung
A curtain of cloth caps and tripes between us,
You determined in your missionary zeal
I with a subtle plan for a seduction.
Against the gorgeous month you spent in Rome
I set wet weekends on the pier at Whitby.

We talked, my God we talked and all the time,
My clumsy farmer's fingers hurt your soul.
The suit I wore, a smart new Co-op check
Paid a poor dividend compared to daddy's.
The night crept on, my bones embalmed in gin
Grew less insistent in their urge for sin.
You were too nice, too earnest and too kind
For the crude, virile game I had in mind,
I was too moral, tired, bored and mean
To keep you from your *London Magazine*.

Police Description

Measured heel to head I register
Six feet one inch with a nude foot.
My weight, thirteen stones, kept in the middle
From riotous expansion by a steel and canvas belt,
Socially a right and proper distinction.
I suffer in the flesh under the accepted sins:
Lust, greed and tyranny wage an unending war
Within my bowels and boundaries,
I have my erections and my crucifictions,
Despair and sometimes a tiny candle of triumph.
In this very desirable property
With its fertile gardens and thick woods
I live in a small room with two little windows.
Crouched in this bedsittingroom I spend my days,
Seldom venturing into my estate.
To every face I meet I make my demand,
"For Christ's sake reconstruct me with love."

Fountains Abbey

We start as all the popular programmes start
With the commercials at the gate, the picture postcards,
Presents, films, the omnipresent lolly
Clutters up our history with our past.
In natural sequence to the world of commerce,
Authority demands its twentieth of a poem
To let the inheritors view their heritage.
All formal rites performed we now are free — to enter
And wander down to where a restless river
Fails to bear all our sins away.
There in the soft green meadow, mellow in the sun,
Stone upon prayer upon torn finger nail feels for the heavens
And crumbles in its own inadequacy.
My daughter asks, how many men have died
Creating this high monument to pride?
God knows! If all the men who died in its defence,
Were laid — with proper reverence — side by side
Within its longest shadow, this shallow valley
Would be levelled to its highest hill.
And still they come the concubines of truth.
The machinist, standing on the Abbot's tomb,
Baring her teeth into the camera's eye,
Has poised stiletto heels above his heart,
And in the infected blood the world may see
The adumbration of its history.

Please Don't Laugh

I have given up trying to be grown up
And spend my time in adolescent joys:
Finally thrown my "I am Jesus" face off
And gone out to the boozer with the boys.

13

One time I took my stand a little distant
Listened to their jokes and felt superior,
Quivered at the mention of a pair of tits,
Coloured from my toe to my posterior.

For many years I looked round for a model
And two or three times thought I had found one,
But when I tried to pin them down for study,
A boy remained, I found the man had gone.

The first one had a pride that stank like mine did
The second had a nibble with a tart,
The third one curried favour with the wealthy
The fourth, poor sod, became obsessed with art.

One more said that he would pin his faith in love
To rid the world of adolescent strife,
But quickly called me outside for a punch-up
When some kind neighbour said I'd jumped his wife.

My mother thought the world was growing rotten,
That God would take His loved ones for His own
— Perhaps that's why I sometimes feel so lonely
Playing blues records on the gramophone.

Last week I went out walking in the country
And heard the turtle-dove call from a tree,
I didn't stop to listen to his love-song
I knew he wasn't singing it to me.

As I came home I had to pass a cripple
I thought I ought to smile as I went by,
"Now there's someone that you should try and love, son",
I walked straight past, I couldn't meet her eye.

A candidate for office came to our house
"Just look and see, sir, what my party's done",
I pointed to a block of flats like barracks
And trees that stood there weeping for the sun.

Kind Dr Best's the one who'll cure my sickness
In his still waiting-room I sit and pray,
He'll give me Soneryl to help the night on
And heart-shaped Drinamyl to cheer the day.

So farewell to the purple-headed mountain
The family house, the river running by,
Exotic over-ripe fruits in the winter
The atom bomb that lightens up the sky.

O Father will you cross my brow with water
And place my tired hands upon my chest,
Remove my testicles and their appendage
And teach me how to love with what is left.

Exercising the Dog

Green fingers float in the air,
Under a flawless sky
The dying flowers walk,
Summer eyes impale me.
   Discipline the hand
Keep the mind on gardens
Deny in silence all the spoken lies,
Smile at strangers.
   O gentle, tender heart
   Bless this warm salt tear
   Furnish an empty room.
Tongue to beseeching tongue
Perform the evening sacrifice
Add emphasis with words
Move down the tightening thigh
With rapacious hand
Manipulate the nipple
   O Lord Jesus grant me this night.

A Beginning

Turning the pages of your magazine
Your tiny mind blurred by this modern dullness
You see that trees are wood and water wet.
Marvel at this my young friend while you may,
For one day you will wake to find that trees
Are question marks or figures of reproach
And piping in their bare and barren branches,
Or singing songs of sorrow in the spring,
Ex-angels of the Lord speak of lost heaven.
Then you will find your thoughts will turn to water,
That special liquid from the crystal stream,
No longer water but the grace of God.
How can you mix water with that rancid joy
That sees a tree as wood and water wet?
I thank you Lord for my uncertainties.

Evensong

You ask "what has gone wrong,
Where are the day's soft touches
And evensong?"

You sigh for urgent hands
For flustered blood-filled faces
And promised lands.

Time was when urgent feet
Were felt in the waiting flesh
Far down the street,

When we so full of fire
Performed our night oblations
In day attire,

Feeling it not remiss
To ease the pressures with a
Clerical kiss

Indiscreet in a room
Where antelopes are poised
And roses bloom.

Why, my dear, could you not be
Content with possessing the
External me

But hanker in your heart
For that rich pearl with which
I cannot part.

Trapped in the flesh and bone
The light of the world watches
And weeps alone.

Plea for a Decent Death

There are corners of this town
Where I have no wish to die;
Outside the Salvation Army Citadel
For instance, or in the cheaper shopping centre.
To come face to face with my Maker
After carefully stage managing
My disastrous and unsuccessful life,
Dressed in a Burtons suit, in a setting
Unworthy of my ambition
Would be high farce or great tragedy,
Something I have spent a lifetime avoiding.
Can one look at death objectively?
The trouble is one is so terribly involved.
From the slimy skinned rabbit
Making its first and formal protest,

To the shambling, backward looking reprobate
Regurgitating his old sins,
One and all are committed to death.
So when I die let me die with dignity
On Saturday, bathed and wearing a clean vest,
Unloved perhaps and unmourned
But with a paid up policy
And walking in the "nicer" parts of town.

All Had Seemed Propitious for the Harvest

All had seemed propitious for the harvest
The winter frosts had broken down the clay;
Safe in the barn the seed was bagged and dressed
Ditches were dug, the sun shone all the day;
Last year the orchard had been pruned for fruit.
Only a lack of brains distinguishes the brute,
I had forgotten my fine flesh would decay.
Trichomoniasis in the bull
Was just bad luck,
All the abortions were to be expected.
The wire worm that caused a second sowing — that failed,
It happens all the time,
One learns to bear one's losses with philosophy.
After the favourite heifer died of bloat —
We sacked the cowman!
But still we had mastitis and a burnt-out barn.
Yet the harvest was good according to the baker,
Neighbouring farms were yielding fifteen sacks to the acre
And they were simple men.
  Begging for water from a wealthy see,
  Crying to a steely sky for mercy,
I sold my farm to a stockbroker.
Now I have ceased to grow
I would be happier living in a city.

Snobs

When you asked
To ease a prolonged silence,
"What would you like to be?"
And I replied,
Being oppressed by boredom,
"A rich man"
You were kind enough to laugh.
But should I treat the truth
With the recklessness it deserves
And say
"Dead"
You would play Harrods
To my Woolworths.

The Guns of Navarone

We sit in isolation
The last remaining twenty in the world.
Country women waiting for a bus
A lady of the town in search of sleep
The unemployed, an old man after warmth.
We seek the reassurance of a world
More beautiful than ours, where men
Are brave or bad, handsome or unworthy.
Where morality consists of simple phrases
Taken from our childhood reading.
"He did his duty," lives right to the end
Or dies a hero's death. We listen to the same thing
Every Sunday, without this colour or glory:
Without this Vistavision screen:
Without the slickness of the steel guitar
Allowed a moment to enthrall with "Chinatown".
The lights are dimmed. The white dressed waitress
Feels for and finds her normal face.
We start with smoke trailing behind an aircraft's belly,

A bleeding finger drawn through clear blue water.
With such dramatic skills the heroes are assembled
And set in motion for our entertainment.
The bearded guest star makes his brief appearance,
Fierce faced and aggressive in the gut.
But we are not deceived, we know this man of old,
His heart holds great compassion
For the splendid chaps he sends off to their doom.
In both our worlds the unpleasant must be done,
And sympathetic men are hard to find.
Who could wish for more than being mourned?

Now the plot divides into different scenes.
The journey over sea, the spy, the storm.
Ship sunk upon a harsh, unfriendly shore.
Sea that storms and stuns the battered boat
Swallowing its meal in one gigantic bolt.
Only the guns and ammunition are saved,
And rightly so, for now we deal in death,
Here life has one finality, the end —
Performed with knife or gun. The camera feeds
Itself upon the spreading smear of blood.
Have pity for the belly that must bear
The defecation, gripped and twisted
By this defloration of the flower of love,
It begs to be excused. Into this turbillion
Of truth, the gentle ones are kicked with savage boot.
The toadstool lifts its crude and brutish head,
Two selves are gratified, satisfaction is all.
Surely one is sacrificed for you, my fellow watchers?

And all the time the target for this exercise,
The twin guns, glower over the sad sea.
Underground, beneath the mountain's crust,
They sit and stare, idle in a world of busy men.
The Mediterranean sunshine
Has not mellowed this destructive pair.
The warm air and the wine, the simple living
Cannot corrupt these intellectual giants.

Only the odour of corrupted flesh
Can end their iron interjections.
The plot unfolds, murder proliferates.
Men, throwing up their hands in praise
Or imprecation, fall like palsied puppets.
Or in slow motion slide, surprised and hurt,
Over a bridge or down a cruel cliff.
Pity the men who find no rest in mother earth,
Denied her womb for all eternity
They wash about the oceans and the seas,
Unredeemed in dissolution.
    One German is allowed some human feeling.

As it was ordained in the beginning,
The heroes breach the fort. Then starts the final scene.
The fight to fix the fuses, camouflage the plastic bombs,
Lay to view the obvious red herring — all against time.
Now the end is near the speed increases.
The fleet is seen. Five destroyers steaming for the gap.
In the hollow of our hearts we feel
The monstrous thunder of indifference,
As the two proud penises ejaculate
Their horrid semen.
Once — twice,
And then the mountain top bursts into flowers.
The whole world is transformed,
As multi-coloured petals, stained with blood,
Float through the holocaust
Into a sea engaged in other business.

It is enough.
A comrade's handshake, a cigarette,
A good man's love for a good woman,
And we are released into the sunshine.
    Treading assuredly on the zebra crossing
    We walk once more the emptiness of life.

Woman in Harrogate

She walks with a reserve
Learnt in a husband's bed.
Her eyes take in my shabbiness
And reject me
Focusing again the empty air.
  Breasts that cry for comfort,
Graceless dignity,
And sad respectability.
  As we pass,
In a ferocity of perfume,
Sense is annihilated.

Man in Harrogate

So full of fire and fury
This tiny Jewish Griffon
His lust shoots out in slashes
From the iron that he spits on,
Seven generations of tailors have not made
This bundle of passion a lover of his trade.

Not for you eternal moments
When inarticulate tongue
Stutters the glorious words
God sends the simple and the young,
The dream loses its clarity, the hope grows old
O cut a coat to shield you from the coming cold.

Questions Are Easy

The Sabbath envelopes me
With sad and military sounds.
An eleemosynary cat treads its way
Through the jungle of an unshorn lawn
Its ears pricked to the violence
Of my neighbour's wet and windy daughter.
I hate looking out of windows,
The broken pane, flaking paint
The squalor of my garden
Reproach the vanity of my dreams.
Upstairs my only decent suit hangs
Reserved for the working week,
Which distracts me with boredom
And leaves me shabby on Sunday,
Leaves me shabby on Sunday
And silly in a miserable household.
Two doors away the bald old man
Who won the bowlegged woman
Walks with a longer stride —
Because he wrote posterity in sperm!
Can love wear a ridiculous hat
And stand on a frosty pavement
Shivering with the lecherous stars?
Can love rise above the waistline
And still lay for eleven plus exams
At seasonal and irregular intervals?

Questions are easy, the smallest child
Quickly learns the trick asking with serious face
"What's that thing that hangs between the bull's legs, Mr Ashby?"

Questions are easy.
Disconcerting dear to find I hurry home
Like any rabbit to its hole,
Though I profess contempt for how we live
And should I find you out
Feel such an emptiness and shock.
Answers are sometimes surprising.

Middle-aged Romance

"Admit it now, I behave like a callow boy,
Dogging your footsteps, hanging around your door,
Waiting at corners for a word or smile;
What an absurd, lugubrious figure of fun."
This morning in the mirror, confronted by a face
Wrinkled, bleary-eyed, teeth tart, nose all askew
I could have laughed — though the joke is an old one —
Laughed at its arrogance and coy conceit.
"Oh ho," I thought, "at it again you lecherous old bastard
You fancy once again the romantic role.
The electric shock of accidental touches,
The soft eyes on a soft night in a soft spring,
Mesmerized by hands and an untidy desiring."
God forgive me Keats, but this is the stuff
That poems are made of in these enlightened days,
Beauty and truth is "strictly for the birds".

Dead Fish

"The swallows with their sharp neurotic cry
Remind me the urgent hours are passing by,
A poem cannot breathe and grow
In a town that lies asleep
Where love and virtue are so cheap."

I could have wished that this had not been said
Her words float round my ears fish long since dead
And swill about the beaches of my mind
With all the flotsam I have left behind.
   Her intellectual pretensions were
   By far the least developed part of her.

Forsaken Drawing: for Betty

This elongated horror
Was conceived as beauty.
A model of colour
And regal dignity.
With luck, perhaps, Mummy,
At least a Fairy Queen.
But something went awry,
The left eye, it was mean,
Had a persistent cast.
The mouth smirked with a sly
Malignancy, and past
The window a fresh start
Was offered on roller skates.
But you can't leave your heart
My love, that one equates
The I, corrects visions,
Doubts all your loves and hates,
Questions your decisions.

A Few Lines for Old Jim, the Timekeeper

Last night, card clocked and ready for cleansing
From the day's dullness; passing our ritual joke
About a smell of snow in the air, you
My late puppet-master uttered your last words.
"Another quarter and I'll be up the road."
Well Jim, time was passing quicker than dinner hour
And you ran out of road. The warning bell
Ended your dreams of tomorrow, the final whistle blew,
Who but a tiny handful gave two hoots?
The clock still ticks, the hooter blows its great Amen,
But you, old sharer of our sorrows, can lie in late.

My Poor Darling

My poor dear
Sitting here,
Dreaming,
In an old coat,
Before the freshly lit fire.
Before dawn
Is quite born,
And night snuffed his candle
And dog end of desire.

My poor dear
Sitting here,
"Stale Every Morning",
The aspirin and hot tea,
If only!
I'm lonely!
Burnt shame and hard boiled pride
And the eternal me.

My poor dear
Sitting here,
If we pray — forgive us
Could, would our dull hearts sing
Like the bird
That we heard
Twenty years ago this spring.
 O my poor darling!

Love Poem

She with a beauty still unblemished.
Time they say has been unkind,
Her eyes swim in a sea of sorrow
Her skin hangs on an old shame,
They are pleased with their sense of pity.

This morning, with a flat face,
Breakfasting on a Beethoven Sonata
Giving your mind to madness
You pursued a non-existent argument
To an irrefutable end.
   Outside, the sun sparkled on wet grass
Splashed with light the apple blossom,
A stupid tree cried, "God be praised!"

You looked into your yawning hell and wept.
I have no pity left to put into your hand,
The bare skin shows beneath the hair of love.
But should I find enough
To take your thin, tired throat between my hands
And squeeze the breath of death into your form,
Out of the agony of an eye
Filled with dreadful accusations
You would weep,
   "This, my love, when life is sweet!"

Attempted Suicide

I have laboured in your vineyard twenty years,
Squeezing the grapes of love until what's left
Is sludge and sediment.
The vats are empty though we both still tread
With desperate feet the fruitless skins of love.
The heart is numb with self inflicted wounds,
The body falls which ever way it fancies.
As the salt and spittle bubble on your lips
I am consumed in an involuntary yawn.

Cuckoo

He looked with intermediate eyes
Along the lineaments of her thighs.

Man's history was just a fleeting
Moment that led to this lovers' meeting.

Standing around incurious cows
Watch importunate hands invade her blouse.

The limpid air is bean blossom sweet
And her sunlit hair is a field of wheat.

The minor animal creation
Ignore this momentous copulation.

A cuckoo whistles its ribald sound
To the lovers stretched on the stony ground.

Marriage

Marriage held together
In the warmer weather
By cold social duress,
God finds it hard to bless.
There is no joy for me
Or you that I can see
In burning all our boats,
Cutting each other's throats,
Yet share out all the blame
The shame is still the same.
Under a field of stars
Why is it only Mars
Comes up with an answer,
Where is my own Cancer?

However much the head
May justify the bed,
The lymph between the thigh
Increase and fructify,
At some time one must start
To celebrate the heart.

For Suki Dara

You sit and survey your jolly kittens
As they dart about like minnows on the floor.
Unconcerned with naughtiness, you tolerate
Their mischief, ignore their breaches of good taste
Until they nip your nipples or use their claws
With more vigour than discretion
Then you deal them an uncompromising swipe
That allows no misunderstanding of your position.
Yet we had begun to fear the stars
The time and the right Tom would never be in conjunction.
Always that useless Ginger sod hanging around
Never seemed to have the tool to finish the job.
Yet what he lacked in potency
He made up for in persistency
Ploughing through snow and frost, to rendezvous
With you on the kitchen window sill.
His habits there left much to be desired
But the children fell for his wistful devotion line.
   Old black Tom called just once
   There was no need to call again.
   Moral, — Love is piercéd hearts on walls
         But romance is a load of balls.

In the City

Now, before I know you,
While the eye is uncertain
And the eradicable warmth
Permits a pleasure in your face.
Now, while the blood
Makes its extravagant promise
The residual fires
Express a mild desire,
Let us predict the predictable
Chart the vulgarity of experience.
We could meet in a city
Which would not pass judgement.
In the amoral streets —
Guts held in a clenched fist —
Suffer the ache for knowledge.

    And should we learn from this,
This worried insemination?
Should we, when what comes between us
Resumes its languid posture,
Know the truth of one another?

In the Strict Sense

In the strict sense of a strict word, poetry,
This hardly is a poem.
It has no formal shape
No subtle rhythm, no discipline in fact.
It is the reflection of a reflex action,
An attempt to describe the complexities
Of a relationship outside the accepted code.
    You will agree, I know, that externally at least
Meeting in a rather squalid room
Presided over by a British Railway urn
Is not conducive to the wilder passions.

The whole point is however that we meet
And by this simple act of innocence
Become involved in conflicts
That tear the heart in two.

   Tonight I was late again!
Saw you from across the track
And found my feet taking the steps
Two at a time.
Felt pretty bad about this;
To see you desperately feigning interest
In notice board and indicator
Filled me with sorrow and despair.
I have become so stupid I forget
The simple acts of common thoughtfulness.
Forgive me.
   One certainty in an ever changing world
Is the battle for a table and two chairs,
That and the indifference of the coffee —
Which I never seem to taste.
Tonight you have remembered your father's paper
Having all the virtues of a dutiful daughter.
I wish I could forget the sullen clock,
The bus, the crowds that jostle at our shoulders.
Never get the time somehow
To ask you all the questions
That chase around my lonely mind at midnight.
About the other time you were engaged,
What happened, where was it and how long ago?
You realize by now I'm very nosey.

   You are such a normal person
I cling to your commonsense
Making demands that are no doubt unfair.
Do I then use you for my own ends?
Are you too kind to say the benediction
To an affair with no apparent future?
Do I offend against one of God's little ones?

Enough,
The time is twelve,
The children are asleep,
Tomorrow has his foot firm in the door.

Roundhay Park: for Joyce

Snatching an illicit hour together
Happy to be anywhere at all
We look, eyes soft with love,
At the washed out roses.
"This" you say, pointing
A tarnished bud, "is Peace."
And this is true, for peace
Is always threatened at the edges
By a headache and tomorrow
Or a quick touch of hands
A muttered goodbye, a wave
And a bus disappearing in the dusk.

Poetry

Poetry is not making up stories
With pretty phrases and happy endings.
It does not seek to show a world
Of beautiful beasts
Serenely strolling through pleasant pastures;
It does not seek to show cool reason
Dominating the human situation,
How could it?
In fact there is so little left
To write a poem about these days
That I can visualise a time,
Not too far distant,

32

When the breed becomes extinct.
Take the spring or last winter (any offers?)
Take birth and death
And the ever popular copulation,
They have all been done,
Done to death.
Or again, pike are popular
And all the tiny creatures
At the bottom of my garden,
Flies and frogs, even compost heaps
Have had their moment of glory.
    But now the fishermen and DDT
Are building a new and better world.
All that remains amiss
Is that old reprobate the human heart,
And even that they tell me is coming along nicely.
Anytime now an anti-guilt pill is expected
Which will alter for all time
The whole nature of the poem.
Then we can expect the modern Lawrence to write
"Glory is of the camshaft
And down its magnificent nuts and pinions."
When the great day comes
Who knows, Jesus might merely be an oilcan.

What You Are

What you are, you are, so don't complain
A twig that twitches over water
A figure seen upon a screen
And worn for half an hour
Or sometimes, not so often, what you see
My eyes say, what they think you ought to be.
And for the rest, standing under God's rain
A conscious being, awkward, dull and plain.

Budgerigar

How like the human type you are my pretty bird,
You speak but what you say are words that you have heard,
Shouted or cooed into your ear until you find,
They slither off your tongue, but never reach your mind.

Sunday Morning Lie-in

"What is the matter?" you said
Turning a tired head
On a dishevelled sheet,
The question was indiscreet.
To temporize I asked you "why"
Unaware that you had heard me sigh,
Surprised my tiny exhalation
Should cause you more than irritation,
How could I say "I wish that you were dead"?
This is the sin that holds the heart in fee
For every hurt one tries to make amends
After all, we had been more than friends,
I stumble down and make a pot of tea.

The State of the Union

She
   "I never intended —
We were such good friends!"

He
   "What is said is not intended
To have precise meaning
Or to be believed.
What the eyes reveal

Or the breasts suggest
Finds an ache in me.
Given a suitable night,
Warm, a traditional moon,
Reflection only on the lake,
After the fingers find the nipple
In the gentler preliminaries
The legs automatically open!"

She
   "A relationship between
Two differently constructed bodies
Always ends . . ."

Fingers

Fingers can poke and pluck
Can pinch and prod,
Cleanse the nose and soul
Of dirt and sin.
Fingers can lie white worms
Upon a velvet couch.
Fingers can fumble in a feverish frenzy
Where the censor's mind
Would hesitate to enter.
The common view is that the mind
Controls the movement of these five,
This is, of course, not true,
Or looking at them now
I am all evil.
If I take a cleaver
And with a clean, quick stroke
Sever them at the knuckle
To lie five bleeding stumps
Upon the table,
Is my offence removed?
She has two hands that tear my heart in two.

A Tiny Scar?

Love is a thorn and can catch
Grasping fingers when they snatch
To claim the chosen rose.

Love is only understood
When a ragged smear of blood
Her rigid terms impose.

Rose and thorn, a tiny scar,
Show my darling just how far
We have come to where we are.

And They Came to a City

Ironic one should find the seeds
Of any sort of love in Leeds,
Or feel the heart exposed to pain
In areas round Vicar Lane,
Where I remember as a youth
The flesh becoming quite uncouth,
Pressed in the doorways of cheap shops
Hands confused with buttons and pops.
For it was hard at seventeen
To find oneself caught in between
Two wars, living in a city
One could neither love nor pity.
So this clandestine pilgrimage
In what is called maturer age
Holds undertones of problems we
Did not find answered by Paul Klee,
Or local intellectual scribes
With vitriolic diatribes.
One must assume that no one man
Can milk the stars into a can,

Or place his finger on the spot
That's troubled him from the year dot.
When love sets up its row of fences
Jump and damn the consequences
Or so one mutters to oneself
Prostrate upon a mattressed shelf.
Life shows two roads and one must choose,
Whichever one you take you lose
Some virtue from your meagre stock,
For one cannot turn back the clock
Redeeming all one's indiscretion
With a show of self-confession.

Into your neat, well-ordered life
I bring four children and a wife
A begging bowl and a carving knife.

A Poem about Not Writing a Poem

I could, if pressed, write I suppose
About the beauty of your nose
Although the truth is — dare I tell? —
I don't recall it very well.
Your eyes would make some copy too
I do remember both are blue
And mellow like a well-kept wine
So much superior to mine
Which have a rather shifty roll
Like two fish swimming in a bowl.
Your ears I will assume are there
Incarcerated in your hair.
I should, because it's fair and just,
Describe the merits of your bust,
But this might give the verse a twist
Repugnant to the Methodist.
Therefore between your neck and feet
I shall be moral and discreet,

I'll not remark your charming grin
Is there a hint of double chin?
Perish the thought, the man's a beast
Who when confronted with a feast
That's perfect to its seventh course
Would quibble at the brandy sauce.
Your hands still give me quite a fright
They look so helpless, cold and white
I'd worry if you didn't take care
To wrap up in the cold night air,
Or if your tongue when in full spate
Forgot the last time that you ate!
But since I am yours to command
I'll discipline this errant hand
Before it gets quite carried away
And mentions things it shouldn't say.
From me no moral dereliction
To titillate the "women's section",
No Eve, no Adam and no fall
In fact I'll write no poem at all.

At the Right Time

Never believe the day will fall
Exactly as you want it to.
Imperfections start with the child
Disciplined upon its pot
When sun and sounds insist
That joy is waiting
In playroom or green garden.
    So all through life the event
Is never timed to meet the need.
And love is no exception to the rule,
Makes an oasis in a happy desert,
Agitates the womb, asks, and sometimes gets,
Impossible feats of endurance.

If love has laid its finger on your heart
Take it — or travel to a far country.
Whichever way you'll find the fever burn
As sure as night will find you twist and turn.

O Do Not Speak

O do not speak
Do not say a word.
Day breaks with glass on stone,
Fingers fumbling for yesterday's pain,
The familiar bitterness of living.
    But now, while your eyes still hold
A certain integrity,
In this fragile peace
Set in a hostile soil,
    Do not speak
O do not say a word.

A Cold Wind

I have seen your face all week;
Following with my eyes in streets and stores
The most unlikely strangers.
And though I told myself
"Don't be a fool", the hope persisted.
Today, on your return
I scuttle rabbit-like from work
To find your bus has gone!
    Suddenly, no one is like you,
The street is filled with faces dull and sullen,
From the east a cold wind blows.

Lovers

"Do you love me?"
Sooner or later the question must be asked,
Or smouldering in some corner of the mind
It grows to such a pitch of feverish doubt
The mind itself is burnt up by the flame.
So out it comes,
Whispered over the coffee cups
Or teasingly while shivering in the cold.
   The answer hardly ever satisfies,
"Sometimes: not now: yesterday"
And with private reservations one says "yes".
So though I know that words are only words,
And what your true eyes tell me must be true,
"Darling, do you love me?"

Come O Lord

Come like winter sunshine
Or the Christmas rose,
Come as frost on the lawn
Or the dancer's pose.

Come as sudden death
Or as a turning head,
Come as shyly as sleep
When words have been said.

Come as sorrow to joy,
Like a daughter's smile
Or come with the warmth
Of a lover's profile.

40

Come as rain, come as sleet,
A smile in the street,
Come as noise or silence,
Come as peace or violence,
But come Lord come.

Down — by the Old Millbank

Sunlight on the Thames
Has its own particular virtue.
The buildings like decaying shark's teeth,
The Lowry figures, walking on awakening grass,
Placate the critical eye.
   If life was as innocent as a springtime afternoon,
And yesterday's anger left the veins unpunctured.

   O fragile happiness
That shatters at the impact of a shadow,
Making me tread with unaccustomed care
Around the fragments of a harsh experience.

Reductions

The conversations of minor civil servants
Are tedious and very long;
What one does with begonias,
The proper way to lay a concrete path,
The stupidity of the unemployed.
One smokes a cigarette,
Feels embarrassed and foolish;
Ignorant of the answers to
Everyday problems of ordinary life.
After robbing the taxpayers
Of five minutes' official teabreak,

One returns to the counter to find
Mr O'Flaherty bibulous and broke,
Whispering for "a wee loan"
To ring his sick mother in Watford.
"Dance me a jig, Mr O'Flaherty,
While I whistle an Irish tune."
"With pleasure" says Mr O.,
And his thin legs dance to my weak whistle.
Suddenly over my shoulder appears
The supervisor's face, code heavy,
Scored through with amendments.
The weak whistle diminishes
To sibilance and silence,
The rheumatic legs stop twitching
My pencil becomes formal and inhuman.

A Few Lines for Mother

A stern lady with a huge hooked nose
Who limped through life one foot set firm in Heaven.
How Grandad put the leaven in her loins
Was not revealed within the *Joyful News*,
But you, my mother, blessed the sacrifice.
For you it seemed so easy to be good
Locked in a close-knit nonconformist world,
But when I shed my soft and shallow sins
I felt no guilt before the eyes of God
But found your sorrow more than I could bear,
Lying in bed in terror at the thought
That you might die and leave me all alone.
"Too close for comfort", now the rebel cut
With one sharp stroke the last remaining cord
Leaving his mother's house not to return.

My first true love so thwarted in your plan,
Forgive God, if you can, the sins of man.

London

There is little in this frenzy
That concerns the human heart
And the daily Crucifixion
Can be the only thing worth living for.
  Inserted in a tube and shot
Like shit into the sea
One enters the city and sinks
Into obscurity, or finds,
If vested with morality,
Scope for such eccentricities
As writing verse, or
Calling toil a form of service.

Returning each night upon the tide
To desolate suburbs
Where love dribbles away
In loneliness in pubs,
Staring at inert hands
Through alcohol dulled senses.

Legs by Dictionary Definition

"Toes", an alliterative ten, overlapping,
Screwed tight during the tossed away
Hours of a thoughtless night.
"Toes", "trodden on", or "on which to tread",
But they "never toe the line".
  The "instep", which is always "falling"
From Grace, "out of step" with society,
Never springing to attention when
The forelock needs a tug.
  "Heel", which when in love last year
I was "head over", and "behaved like".
"A vulnerable part", I am often
"Down at", "come to", or on occasions "cool".

43

When the times get tough
I show "a clean pair of".
   "Ankle", a rum joint where I have been "twisted",
"Sprained", "strained", and "fettered".
At times has "good connections".
   "Knee", and "thigh", which is you and I
Or grammatically, you and me,
"Bony", yet "easily bruised",
"Soft", and "occasioned to cramp",
Which my hand impulsively reaches for.
   "Knees", which still refuse to kneel
To One whose feet I am unworthy . . .

Ask a Silly Question

I have been unwell for some time,
Since the magnolias blossomed,
And now the hay harvest is over
Combines consume the cornfields.
   Being unable to decide
The simplest details of living
What to have for lunch,
When or where to marry.
Having annoyed my friends with tactless letters
And lost the knack of writing poems,
Nothing remains, for the religious man, but prayer.
So I have bombarded the Lord
With pleas for mercy and guidance, without result,
Until this morning when, asking
"Lord what shall I do?"
The answer came — GO TO DUNSTABLE!

Never

The footsteps that are never yours,
Knock upon the door never you,
Never the letter where my feet are wiped.
The red coat never wrapped around
Your never violated body.
The telephone number never forgotten.
My never revealed excursions
Never suspected by my ever loving.
The man who was never me
Never loved by the never loving
Woman who was never you,
Never being more than my imagination,
Which day after day never forgets
Your never developed breasts, and sighs
For the consummation of a never intended affair.

Tidal Waves

Being in a moral sense old-fashioned
The similes I use will not confuse you,
The earth and moon. Like us
Two disparate bodies seeking similarities.
Without will and unable to resist
You draw my tides and leave my sand exposed
To waste and sun, the foot of man and bird.
I send exploratory rockets to your atmosphere
Seeking a landing on your foolish heart,
And find there that the mechanism of love
Shatters upon the edges of your rocky mind.
Or should I, by scientific expertise,
Succeed in circling you and bring
My missile back to its home base,
It comes back as a singing bird or thunder.

45

The Arthritic Tree on Otley Bridge

In Otley, the arthritic tree,
The first time that you went with me,
Was naked to the winter's waste
And too distorted for your taste.

The bridge stepped over in one span
No longer than the life of man,
And on its farther bank there stood
Man's sin portrayed in tortured wood.

Its fearful shape disturbs my mind
Though twelve fine summers lie behind.

Poem

I say this will pass in a day
And tomorrow feel the same way.
Or the pain will die in a week
Yet the tears still run down my cheek,
And seem like to be there
Until the end of the year.
Yet a relief to find
I still retain an analytical mind
And with a little effort can take apart
Your head, untouched vagina and your heart.
If I may say, and cause you no offence
My first impression was your innocence
And to be frank I felt a certain pity
For your self-evident inadequacy.
Your eyes showed worry, mouth was most unsure
Your breasts and understanding immature,
It was unnecessary to reveal soul
To one who merely asked you for the dole.
But then the blemish could be blamed on me
Who could discover sorrow in a tree

46

Or feel a joy that caused the blood to thrill
At baroque vases and a daffodil.
Happy the man oh happier by far
Who understands the belly of his car
And over half a pint becomes ecstatic
About acceleration in the traffic
The ruthless hand of God will never touch his head
Enter his toilet or defile his bed.

Leeds No.2

The trams would grind up Beeston Hill
Until well past midnight,
Squealing to a halt at Tempest Road
Then moaning along the cemetery
Into Beeston. Passing the pub
Where the barmaid — early Women's Lib —
Had given up wearing a bra.
At sixteen years of age I would drop pennies
Over the counter top to see her tits
When she obligingly bent down.
   Dad's canaries would start to sing
Around five o'clock, so the nights were short.
By pulling the scrotum over the penis
You could almost persuade yourself
The itch between the crutch was imagination;
Though the stains on the sheets were biological enough
And were of course never talked about.
   Sometimes we had a fitness fad
Walking through the grime to our window
Dressing jobs, believing we were breathing in fresh air.
At least we were chained at work
And did not have the time to think of life.
Did we realize we were alive?
The shop smelt of stale sweat and powder,
Armpit solicitations from a thousand women.
We used to laugh a lot because

47

We were too dulled to recognize sorrow.
Apart from death and a few cripples
Scrounging coppers outside Boar Lane Church
Nothing moved us as much as a good film.
Cooper, Cagney, Jean Arthur and Edward G.
Provided our view of reality.
　　At ten p.m. on Saturday
We slipped our leads and ran for home
Tired, dirty and dismayed about we knew not what.
Sunday, twice at chapel, sat upstairs
With Wally, eating peanuts. Reading
The Thriller, or making the choir girls laugh.
Once I smoked a fag during the prayer.
The congregation, retaining their seats and bowing
Their heads, looked as though they were
Engaged in a communal shit.
I could not honestly say that I was saved.
　　As for culture, a copy of
The Good Companions lay about the house.
I knew one poem,
"A garden is a lovesome thing", God, what
A load of rubbish. Strange,
I was not aware men still wrote poetry,
We would have thought it was unmanly.
My heart had not been hit, hurt or harassed
By any art. I liked Billy Bennett
At the Empire, now both levelled to the ground.
Somehow, I do not remember how
Or where, at the age of ten
I became a jazz fan and would cry
At Armstrong's West End Blues, and think
This weakness a barrier from my friends.
On four and nine a week I managed
To start collecting records and confirmed
My father's notion that he had whelped a fool,
Which I now realize was true,
Though at the time I did not think
In relative terms, but black and white.
My vanity made me unsure whether
I was on show in the windows

Or the clothes and dummies.
   Standing watching Burton's and the Fifty Bob Tailor's
Cutters — shabby and consumptive looking —
Parading the streets for a shilling a week rise
Jolted my youthful conservatism.
And the first feel of a woman's cunt
Found my pinstriped trousers unprepared.
Was I growing up and making roots?
   Cricket in Cross Flatts Park until lamplight.
I could run up to the wicket all grace
And lithesome youth, fast and accurate.
At silly point the swallows kept
A careful distance from my hands.
The West Riding recognized beauty
Applauding Hutton's off drive.
   I have returned, but neither Leeds
Nor I have much to say to one another.
The city is cleaned up now. Poets get
Gregory Fellowships for no apparent reason
Apart from the right contacts in high places,
And I have failed to make money,
The only thing Leeds ever tried to teach me.
But I have succeeded in being a failure
And admit the fact — immodestly perhaps.
Sweet Street, where are you now!

St George's Wolverhampton

The shabbiness of the scene
Is not offensive. The social tyrant
Might be affronted by the untidiness,
Being an ordered and disciplined soul,
But as our lives are shabby
And the details of daily living
Untidy, revealing a state of moral anarchy
That the car, Hoover, and cardboard house

49

Prove a poor substitute for,
One could say one was at home.
      Somewhere to live is no problem
To find in the welfare state.
Clinical institutions, sterile and scrubbed,
Reduce the image of God to a filing cabinet,
Love is recognized by its absence.
      Here, refusing to be confined within an ashtray,
Escaping the hawklike duster, it spreads
In untidy profusion throughout the house.
The physical symptoms experienced
Between two differently shaped bodies
Give a momentary illusion of
Unity, concealing the selfishness
Inherent in even satisfied desire.
      But the imaginative love that one receives,
Which is never earned and seldom felt deserved,
Appears mysteriously from the empty air.

For Mother

It was a good day for winter,
Though raining, it was mild
And the soil seemed pleased to receive
The remains of Hilda Harriet Louisa King,
My mother and first lover.
      She died and was boxed on Boxing Day,
Thinking it unseemly, and being too humble
To intrude her death into the Child Christ's Day.
She had lived her latter years
Bewildered by pills and doctors' potions
For kidney, liver and a doubtful heart,
Attending to these matters as best as memory would allow.
      But death, that great impersonator, slyly
Caught her with cerebral thrombosis,
One of the few complaints her
Imagination had not got around to.

50

She did nothing of any importance
And will not be mentioned in the history books.
Reared two indifferent children yet loved them,
Was loyal to one man through force of habit.
Her heart was never weak, her stomach strong,
At loving, few in the Riding could compare.

If we shed tears, forgive us, she has found
Some peace on Stonefalls bleak and stony ground.

Distractions

Your postcards drop to earth
Silent as paper darts thrown in the wind.
They come from where you are, but
Show one views of places you have been,
As if you wished to prove
That life was constant change,
And a relationship could not stand still.
Which I admit is true, although the dead
Are buried now in horizontal posture
Or burnt up at blast off.
   What is written is not what
You wish to say, but a substitute
For words you dare not use.
"Hope you are beginning to pick up,"
Means, "because you left me you must
Be ill, get well soon, darling."
"You really must read Scott
Fitzgerald, you'll recognize
Some of the situations."
This equates my few pints
And your nervous disorders,
With madness of a classic proportion
We neither could presume.
And though I make no answer to your missiles,

For two nights running I have prayed
"Please, God, take this folly from me."
    Only to wake each morning, a murderer
With appetite unimpeded, tramping the lanes
Crying and talking to myself
Of injustice and hate.

Cows

At five o'clock the air is fresh
And pimples one's shirt-covered flesh,
The grass and kale stand firm and true
As soldiers, refreshed by the dew.
The beet is rigid for the hoe
And one can make a better show
At piece work when it holds its pride
Than later when the sun has dried
The moisture from its four-leaved face
And it hangs limp about the place.
This is the fault of Charlie Brick
Who sowed the bloody seed too thick
And will be blamed with vulgar sounds
For robbing day-men of the pounds
Intended to buy fattening pigs,
I hear the "buggers" and the "frigs"!
But Charlie's cunning and he will
Tell all the fault lies with the drill.
But I care "nowt" for drills and ploughs
Having a family of cows
That must be got into the shed
And groomed and washed and milked and fed.
I walk across the cuckoo Pen,
Notice the wires down again.
That's Marigold who scorns the jags
Where other cows respect their bags,
She jumps for clover, gets the shits
Mastitis and two damaged tits.

I shout "come on" and "cupcupcup",
And half the herd gets slowly up
Wandering as blindly to the shed
As man just risen from his bed.
Slowly, heads down, bent nearly double
As full of milk as man with trouble,
Except Suzanne who'll not concur
Until you put your boot in her.
She rises, stands, then coughs and shoots
A stream of shit on to your boots!

For Ann

A woman of quality
Is not created
Whole or wholesome,
And passes through the madness
God prescribes for those
Intent upon eternal knowledge.
   A woman of quality
Learns to lie and cheat,
Becomes an artist in chicanery,
Holding her love like cards
Against her breast
Wanting to trump
Everybody's aces,
Yet never believes she can be loved
And makes demands
Beyond man's frail ability.
   A woman of quality
Learns through guilt
The secrets of the heart,
Wearing her two black eyes
Like bright and shining stars.
   A woman of quality can say
"It was as much my fault as yours,"
And kiss the drunken fist so full of folly.

A woman of quality
Asks for nothing, forgives all
And is imperfect, but aware
In the shattering hours of night
Of the holiness of life.
    The imperfections of man are revealed
When I can no longer love you,
And have forgotten the ecstasy we suffered
Because your neck grows scraggy.
Yet seeing you lost and lonely
In the gaiety of the crowded hall
I am overcome by memories and grief.

For Charles Sisson

Old friend, the spirit
Places us with sundry moves,
Into areas we
Have no wish to be.
And the pattern is laid down,
You stay in the town
Fingering at weekends
The fabric of the countryside:
While I try to compress
The whole of nature into my body
Yet seldom use the eyes
In proper country style
And ache for a town that I despise.

You have little to say to me
And my ears recognize
My mouth's trivialities,
While my pen is incontinent.
Should we meet —
Over the plastic menu
The ritual libation in Guinness
To the fickle muse —

We sit out the long silences
Watching the vulgarity of the masses
In Leicester Square,
Or searching the dustbins
Of our minds for something
We hold in common —
Other than our fallen state.

We have our individual
Brand of happiness and
This does not demand
That our faces express it.
So as you heave your left leg
Forward in characteristic gait,
Your face does not find it necessary
To show excessive pleasure
Or even a mild irritation
As we reconstruct our last
And every conversation.
We do not walk with God,
Though we both know
We cannot walk without Him.
Death is a desirable state
Preferably swift, or should one hope
Mercifully? Not only
Because men are ugly
But the world is too beautiful to bear
And we are constrained
To love the whole
And each and every unpleasant member.
An impossible task
For a warped mind
Combined with an impure heart.

When every day was fine
And innocent treble sang
"You in your small corner
And I in mine,"

Was the vast distance
Between the corners appreciated,
Or how tiny the space
Required to contain us.

After Attending a Poetry Jazz Session

Having been affianced to jazz
Since the age of eight and listened
With a child's grave wonder to Armstrong's West End Blues;
Wept adolescent tears at Ellington,
I viewed with trepidation the meeting
Of an earlier and constant lover
With a later flame, the bitch poetry.
The cultural aura of Crouch End
Is conjured only with the help of alcohol
And the border between sensibility
Where mind, body and spirit are fused in one,
And insensibility, is easily over-run
But on this occasion, passport out of date,
Pocket having no chink for a drink,
The ordeal demanded more courage
Than I can customarily muster.

Whether the jazz being played on entry
Was "avant garde" or "mainstream"
I am unable to say, but Slam Stewart
Played the bass solo thirty years ago.
Ah! the young are unaware that history
Like sin repeats itself "ad nauseam",
Accepting as "meaningful" and "vital"
The washed out words of weary poets
And the crude chords of a barbaric piano.

When the cutting contest began, the musicians
Carved the poets into tiny pieces,
Being professional, masters of their instruments,
Making profounder and more forthright statements
In a clear tone for all to hear.
They reduced the poets to mutterers,
Sighing shaming sins at the confessional.
The unhappy affair on the Serpentine —
That ended in a wet shirt front.
The eccentricity of being out of tune
With the disastrous times one was born in,
Unacceptable in Soho,
Considered gaga in Golders Green.
Where has the son of woman to lay his head?
The undergraduate Milton, blind
But articulate at the bar, where the locals
Listened in amazement to his
Erudite discussion on Arnold.
Or the poetic preacher, guilty
Of three marriages and prouder of this than
Any poem signed by his bankrupt pen.
The final poet, anonymous as a paving stone,
Made remarks, stuttered statements,
As I made my way to the exit.
Not one line remains to please,
Appease or comfort the heavy heart.

I hurry home to my "poems two a penny"
Born out of seventeen years shit-shovelling,
Sired by vanity, a stallion who
Rushes me up most unlikely roads
Hard of mouth, uncontrollable,
Takes the bit between his yellow teeth,
Ignores my feeble pull upon the reins,
Reducing me to an incoherence
Understood by two or three maniacs
Who with loving generosity
See fit to call me friend.
There is beauty in every seen thing,

Rain and cloud, the sun, impersonal star.
Sometimes when absorption with myself
Is broken by a sudden shaft of insight,
For a moment I marvel at grass,
The sound of sparrows, amazed
At a world, grey as this wet Monday.

Impromptu Poetry

I   Shouting for Joy

Lord when I put on a clean shirt
Would you do me dirt?
When I cry
To a grey sky,
"Thank you,"
For having nothing to do,
Would you, loving God
Thwack me with your heavenly rod?
If I learn to lie and cheat,
Scrounge money and the food I eat,
Behave in a million styles,
With alcohol distract my piles,
What the hell can you do,
I still belong to you.

If I join the Civil Service Thou art there,
In my bed, pint pot, bogs, everywhere.
When I touch the virginal tit,
Read the writing on the wall when I shit
All that I view is a reflection of You.
Wonderful are Thy ways,
Unhappy are my days:
In all I see
The world is too lovely.

58

II *Prayer*

As I laid in bed this morning
My hand upon my tool,
I cried "O Lord forgive me
I have been a bloody fool,
Thinking that conversation
With Your August self must start
In some sepulchral chapel
With my hand upon my heart".

Downs and Ups

When I contract my belly in
Defy the mirror with a grin
Yet mark the slackness of the skin
The impact hits me on the chin.

Or drifting in the train to town
Past Ferme Park Up and Ferme Park Down
Although perhaps I act the clown
There's always holly in the crown.

At morning when the dogs of dark
Sit silent, never raise a bark,
I wander Alexandra Park
Praising the Lord, blessed by the lark.

Wingfield Priory

My heart there is a home
Where the mind is easier.
The evening sky, red,
Setting behind hedge and

Paddock gate in the glory
Of the everlasting Light.
Barn with axe cut beams,
The whole demanding
Respect by its very age,
Early Tudor — and my late love.
   It had stood the years so quietly,
Even the birds accepted it
As a friend, and all who
Lived within its plastered walls.
   Winter, when first it
Met my jaded eyes,
Saw ducks sliding on ponds
One of which was
Watering a golden pheasant,
Who flew away, shocked
At man's ill-mannered entrance.
We wandered up and down
In, out and all around.
Evening stole upon us
And found us loath to leave,
Until the frost drove
Us back to London, silent
As sinners before the mercy seat.

   Cap in hand through
Family, foe and friend
I asked for money
And was not refused,
Until it seemed that God
Had found some purpose
For my useless hands,
Or so my vanity assumed.

   Come June I stood
Among the uncut grass,
Guinea fowl cry
"Come quick, come quick,"
Or, "Grey grey grey,"
Echoing all around.

From underneath the eaves
Swallows, swifts and martins
Swooped, flicking across my eyes.
The sky — East Anglian blue,
Shrubs, scents, bees, briars
Were shriven by refining sun.
And should I not weep for joy?

    Surrounded by loved ones,
My study lined with books
Written by my betters,
I sat, fat with feeling
Waiting for words to set me free.
    But from every window
Life set out to distract me.
A blackcap sat upon my table
Questioning my words and motives.
A bullfinch pecked a poppy seed.
A tit, feet fixed in fat,
Swung in a sudden gale
The clock round in a second.
Six cock pheasants called for supper.
A pair of pigeons nested in the barn.
    The days drew to their close
And my paper bore no marks.
    Standing in the ingle-nook,
Looking up the pit black stack
Towards the tiny disc of heaven,
I recognized my failure;
Only time revealed my small success.
But that was after I had run
To a town where the living are stunted,
And one can feel almost one's proper height.

Pets

I am surrounded by pets.
Three caged birds, a cat —
Emasculated, of course —
Two poodles and a dalmatian.
They, the dogs and the cats
Eat food from tins
Filled by an industry
That recognizes a sucker
When it sees one.
The birds, exotic creatures,
Cannot sing; anyway,
What have they got to sing about?
But they utter a few words —
That justifies their captivity.
The mynah bird repeats
"Silly bugger", a proper
Judgement on its owners.
They exist to channel off the love
That cannot be given to
The brotherhood of foolish men.
And of course they never
Disagree or answer back.
I wish someone would
Have me for a pet.
I would sit upon my perch
And the silly things I say
That now annoy, would give such pleasure.
And nobody would expect
Me to say "thank you",
When I pecked your finger
You would think it fun
And not reprove me.

Please, God,
If I can't be a man,
May I be a pet?

Nothing Doing

Nothing drives me back
Neither the sleepless nights
Nor the sprays of May
The things I lack
Or the imagined delights
Of lovers at play.

Along country lanes
Where memories are erased,
Above the petrol fumes, suddenly,
Such scents pierce my nose
That I stand still, amazed
I should have missed
The faintest odour from the earth
Fragrance of the dog rose.
   Dalmatian, dog nose
Grounded over wayside soil,
Stops at my sudden beginning.

Deficiencies

Yours is the culinary triumph
Mine the obese disgrace
I grow so thin in spirit
As I grow fat in face.

For Patrick John Walton
born 4 November 1971

Patrick John Walton, my first grandchild.
Named after two fishermen,
Fourteen days old and unversed still
In the art of casting for compliments.
   We have not met yet. We have the time
But neither of us has the money.
So all I know about you is
The colour of your hair, brown and thick,
And your shoulders are described as
"Like a bull's," which means
Your Grandmama has placed
Her masterprint upon your flesh.
   I was pleased that you were
Disinclined to rush into the world,
Selfishly I must admit
As your mother was growing tired
Of carrying your burden in her belly.
But now we hold in common, besides our sex,
We both are Scorpios,
And I am curious to see
If you handle the problems of living
With greater aplomb and skill than me
Who find life's sting grows fiercer at the tail.
   I feel that I should give you some advice
To help you on your journey to the tomb
But what have I to say? The moon
Is not green cheese, living is rough
And that I think is really far enough.
Besides, I don't think you would wish to know,
I know I never did, I had to learn
Or anyway to live the drama of the days,
Or is it melodrama knocks me out?
   A couple of things I'll mention then I'll close.
Don't mix the grape with grain
The pain is not relieved
By drinking gripewater.
And never let the muse bemuse you

Into trying to write verse
It's hard work, and the punishment
Is greater than the crime.
   Go out into the world as you are now
Naked and in love with everyone.
Lead with your chin.
To hold compassion from mankind
Is the one sin
You should avoid.

Good luck, Pat, if I remember to
I'll send a card each year
And say a prayer for you.

Latter Day Psalms

1

Somewhere there is Grace, Lord,
Was I not told it as a child
When the sound of the sparrow
Filled my heart with delight
And the rain fell like friendship on my head.
   Now the call of the cuckoo
Cannot calm my aching heart,
And my soul is tormented with fear.
   Have mercy, Lord, for I have travelled far
Yet all my knowledge is as nothing.
My days are numbered. Time titters
As I stumble down the street.

Forgiveness, O forgive me, Lord,
Close my critical eye
Take me to your breast
For how else may I die.

2

The tree waves in the wind
But does not break unless
The bough is over-burdened.
When spring disrupts the dead days
Buds, leaves, and birds praise God
In song and silent sound.

  The dead dock, stiff
With last year's pride,
Leans unwillingly in the gale.

  My heart, Lord, is unyielding,
My joints are stiff.
The knuckles of my knees
Refuse to bend.
The knife is at my neck,
My back breaks.

  I will say my matutinal prayers
From a crippled position,
Perhaps the Lord will hear?

3

I lived among lewd men
Beneath the Crouch End clock,
Waiting for God to speak.
But my ears were dull
And what my brain received
My mind misunderstood.
So I took my mean heart to the hills,
Beside the Palace of Alexandra
Gazed on Barbican and grieved.
  Lord speak to me in the morning
  Or the night will be everlasting.
Now all the dogs of Dewsbury
Bay about my heels,
And the foul water of the Calder
Weeps into the sea.

4

On the estate, Lord, the people
Take counsel one with another,
And in the public house
There is lamentation.
The cost of living soars
Like wild duck rising
After morning feed.
Man has neither means nor meaning.
The cry of the young in the street
Rouses a protest in the market place.
　What shall I do, Lord?
Though I bring my sad soul
And place it at Your feet,
My mouth is bitter, for fear
Infects my hand and heart.
The pit of hell yawns wide
Before my floundering feet,
I slip, I slide, I fall,
I try to grasp a skylark
But it flies south for summer.
　My mind is melancholic,
　I cannot praise my maker.

A Stranger in This Land

Lord, I am lonely
And the sun is shining,
Listless, while the wind
Shakes the ageing leaves.
The harvest has been gathered
All is bagged and barned,
Silos burst with grain.
　Why, Lord, must I still stand
Dropping blind seeds
On to a barren soil?

Come, sweet Jesus, cut me down
With the sickle of Your mercy,
For I am lonely
And a stranger in this land.

An Adaptation of a Translation
by C.H. Sisson

What fer do 'e bash me
'Til oi do moan?
I an't said nought 'gen 'im
I an't dun ought 'gen 'im
Jus' talkin' to ole Jim
We was alone.
What fer do 'e bash me
'Til oi do moan?

If 'e doan' let oi be
Oi'll pay 'im back 'e'll see
'E can't do this to me
Or oi'll be goin'
What fer do 'e bash me
'Til oi do moan?

Knows what do raise 'is spunk
When 'e with ale be drunk
Oi'll creep into Jim's bunk
Stark as a stone.
What fer do 'e bash me
'Til oi do moan?

For Rachael

God give you both a gentle child
Unfrightened by the winter's wild
Winds, the baying of the crowd,
The cruel tongues and loud
Lies of ignorant men. Let
Her seek a world where she can find
Food for an innocent mind
And heart. Where she can learn
That when the passions start to burn
The flesh, both lion and dove
Are the true elements of true love.
Pray God, she never may feel shame
For either parent, neither blame
Them for sins common to the world
Before their own flesh was uncurled.
   Let her walk through life as through some cool glade
Where tired and hungry may seek and find shade.

Gone and Forgotten

A piece of land
Where people lived
And died.
Children played
And worry ploughed
A furrow on the brow.
   All gone.
No stone still stands
Or if it does
The remnants of a garden
Hide the ruins.
The cultivated rose
Is running wild
Acacias battle
Through the weeds.

From the straight
Backed ash
A robin sings
A moment, not
In love, but
Celebrating the
Remnants of an
Ill-remembered summer.
　Winter lurks
Just around the corner.

Walking with my Grandchild Rachael in Early Morning

Silence underlines
The punctuality
Of the tractor driver.
A cry from farm
Building and the
Patient cattle's hooves
Crackle over the
Stiff stubble.

Morning mist creates
Phantoms and illusions
Flat becomes upright
Distance loses ground
Plovers and seagulls
Rise from earth
Bound clouds
The cock performs
His work of
Supererogation.

　"Run, Grandad!"
I become the
Entertainer once
Again.

70

Happy Families

You shall not have my dog.
I offered it
And you refused
Because you were afraid,
You shall not have my dog.
He used to read my letters,
Sat in my chair
Touching things on my table
When my back was turned.
I never liked *him*
For the man's a fool
And like all fools
Blown up with self conceit,
Were you so witless
That you had to wed *him*?
You shall not have my dog.
Where are the shelves
He promised to put up,
The rods inside the cupboard
To hang clothes on?
He smells of smoke
And I'm ashamed
To own *him* as
A son-in-law.
You shall not have my dog
To spoil like my grandchildren,
Bed at all hours,
Fretting all day
For sweets and toys,
Touching my books.
Refusing decent fruit,
Asking for more with
Fist still full of food.
Stew in your own juice
And I'll stew in mine,
You shall not have my dog
Not even if you ask.
You shall not have my dog!

71

My Lady

My lady has gathered
Up her purse, said goodbye
And caught the bus to Batley.
I sit in the Little Saddle
Morosely drinking gin,
Thinking of My Lady's
Eyes, sweetness of breath
Breasts like summer roses.
In Market Street, the cars
Snarl at pedestrians
Crossing the road with
Chronic indecision.
Sun drops down winter blue
Life is implacable.
My lady has gathered
Up her purse, said goodbye
And caught the bus to Batley,
A stranger dips his fingers
In her purse.

Langport Poem

I was born
But for what purpose
Time has not made plain
But time, nibbling
Mouselike at my years,
Has left me but little while
To put a meaning
To my father's frenzied moment.
   Once, when I was young,
And life was lovely,
To love the ugly
Help the lame to walk
Was all I wished.

Pity was easy
Compassion came tardily.
   The ideals of the young
One must admire,
Toying with broken bones
And bodies all askew,
Wearing a Christian face
Or a Buddhist attitude
The wickedness of man
Requires but time
To reach perfection.
   But time plays tricks with men.
At thirty I acquired a back
That crippled *me*.
   It never is enough
Good should be done
At best a youthful fancy
Worst an act of pride,
God must be worshipped first.
So I forsook good works
With small remorse
Trying with impure mind
To find pure thought.
   A foolish fancy.
I was aware, I knew
God was about me —
As He is round us all —
But where was the side
To place my finger in?
   Love lost, I labour
At a foolish craft.
My hardening veins
Cry to my fatty heart
Enough!
   Bones not fit for blood
Splinter and crack.
I am alone.
How can I cry
For what I seldom show
My fellow men?

73

Making my foolish marks
On scraps of paper
I foolishly believe
God moves my fingers.
   It is the offertory hymn.
The warden with the bag
Stands waiting at the pew.
But what have I to give
The priest can bless?
A coin
No contrite heart.
   The sun showers blood
Through glass on to the altar
I cannot find the key
A boyish tenor
Or a grumbling bass.
   A cracked bell chimes
The candles are all snuffed.
I hear a voice
"Come, I will give you rest",
But feet refuse to move.

   In the garden
The nightingale
Sings all day
But I am dumb
Nothing to say.
   You, dear friend
Have certainties
God will forgive
The common pride;
There is love in your eye
And a soft voice.
   Perfection is not
   The only key to Heaven.

She Doesn't Sing

She doesn't sing
When I'm sat
In the room.
The whole damn world
Could turn into
The sound of singing birds
Trilling in treble
Booming out in bass
Nightingales
A towering descant.
She doesn't sing
When I'm sat
In the room.

She doesn't laugh
When I'm sat
In the room.
But should I
Take to bed
With boredom or
A hangover
And leave her
Sitting staring
At the box,
Laughter ascends
The stairwell
    And I weep.

Hard Pounding

By breakfast time
Day reaches its crescendo
Hopes explode like
Hand grenades.
I shall plummet

Through somebody's
Back window
And find myself
Face to face
With myself.
O hearts that break
Behind the well-washed curtains
Reject not this man
This enforced
Council tenant
Whose body also
Stretches to
The tightening rack
Of the poor in
Heart and mind.

Survival

A picture window
Over a moody river
Sparkled by sun or
Roughed up by the wind.
A garden, trees
Birds to entertain
If song amazed you.
    A fall of trees
A field to play
The farmer in —
Or Virgil.
    You have worked hard
Hold this in respect,
Not because work is
Worth much, but
Social weight is judged
By the balance in one's bank.
We are all debtors
I owe you

You owe God
The love of whom
Is based on usury.
Pound for pound
We gain an interest
That we never earn.
   Evil is feeling
One is wicked
Beyond the Grace of God
A presumption of
The mad or vain.
I thought I saw your eyes
Warm with love
Hand waving.
Did I imagine what my sad eyes saw?
Was it the sun
Shivering with
Lust upon the earth?
One cannot be sure.

Classic words that stain
A virgin page, dry
Humour, irony
Emotional cowardice
That shudders at
A waiter's trick of trade,
A fear of scenes.

Silent men are
Not immune from
Terror of their neighbours.

In Memory of Lester Young

I never knew the details of his life
Henderson sacked him when he was quite young
Because he didn't sound like Coleman Hawkins
But Basie brought him to New York and made
The famous Lester Leaps In record there.
He blossomed for five years and overcame
The music critics' abuse, but something happened
Solos grew repetitive, his timing went
He was unreliable, forgot his record dates
Or turned up drunk or fell asleep upon his chair.
Like Lowell, his useless work is much admired
And young men seldom listen to his best
Requesting records he would be ashamed of.
Some say the army disorientated him
Others blame it on his being black,
Jazz is always searching for a hero
But being a man's enough to dull your senses.
    I loved him for he made teenage despair
In Leeds, something I discovered I could live with.
He died for our pleasure, doing what he was best at
Blowing upon a reed until he himself was broken.

A Wise Dog

A wise dog
Raises a
Paw when his
God appears.
    Precaution is
The order
Of the day.

78

Lies and Dreams

For Fraser Steel

1

I have visited
This street before
Wandered past the newsagents
Inspected black ties
At an obsequious tailor's
"A sad occasion, sir."
Nodding I place a
Noose around my neck
Finger the material.
    Caught at the supermarket
She stands a supplicant
At my side. Death
And his outriders
Crash across her face
"Did you mind my ringing?"
I shake my head and notice
The weekly fluctuation
Of food prices.

2

That year I did
Not find the Spring
Neither was the
Peace of God
Evident.
    The sacraments were
Observed in Coca Cola;
"Take of this cup, drink
Of the silent masses."
    No one bathed
My suppurating sores
And my heart
was vexed.
Justice and mercy
Were abroad

For the summer.
Beauty was vanished
From the face of the earth.
   I cried
For
The peace of God
Was not evident
And had it been
My evil eyes were
Fixed elsewhere.

                    3

For some months now
I have avoided
The day. Kept at
Bay the light
Lying knee to nose
A writhing lump
Beneath thin rugs
Until night has
Unpacked its stars
And chaos.
   The day is
Too beautiful
For my imagination.
Grass, young girls
Movement of trees
The sun brands
My sad eyes.
   Night and the starlight
Find me at the bar
Or striding empty streets
Clad in a long coat
Dark glasses hiding
Eyes that ask for love.
Never again shall I
Stable that stallion
In my stalls.
   In the ginnel
Underfoot

The glass
Crackles like ice.
   Past Mirfield
Beyond, into
The Pennines
Arterial veins
Run filled
With Sci. Fi. blood.
In this uncharted land
Children learn
From loving parents
How to hate.
   The church stands
On a hump
To reach it one
Must walk through
Sewage farm
Or rubbish tip.
   The House of God
Was built for those
Who fall into the shit.

4

Killkof had not been
Out of late; the word
Was hard, a man was
Going round taking names.
Killkof did not wish
To give his name.
   Idle, at home, the devil
Sat decorously on his shoulder,
He smiled to think a queer
Should have been honoured by a queen!
But this was jealousy, a sad
Complaint common to men of letters.
   The devil never spoke
And seldom thought
What need was there when Killkof
Did both for him.
   "I know a barber's

Where the hair oil flows.
Proprietor and assistant
Men from a warmer clime
Cyprus, a lewd island
Known to Venus.
Their features swarthy
Hair curly and black
Yet all the perfume
Of Arabia
Cannot disguise
The garlic on their breath.
   The atmosphere is
Dignified, a spirituality
Only found in churches
Or urinals.
Little or no
Profanity is heard
One is not asked
To tilt and hold
One's head at an awkward angle,
Quite the reverse, the barber
Holds the untenable position. Or
Should a slight adjustment
Be required, a deferential
Finger points the posture
So desired.
   The snip and clack
Of scissors cutting at
The comb raised hair
Is conducive to a
Softening of the senses.
One can doze in a light
Dream scented sleep,
Sweetened by unguents
Made by ICI,
Safe in the knowledge
No harm can befall."
   Here Killkof hawked
   And spat upon the floor
   The devil sat

His eyes agog for more.
"Should sleep still prove
Elusive, as it can, always
The barber's mirror will amuse.
Wrinkles unnoticed just a
Month before are now revealed,
A fiery pimple cocks
A gangrenous eye.
    The barber concentrating on
His task is unaware
That he is now observed
Pushing his fornicating belly
Into your tingling elbow.
    Let your mind distract
Itself with gels and smells
Lotions, potions, creams and waters.
Notice the warning
DANGER OF DANDRUFF FALL-OUT
Hung from a plastic hook.
Condoms and cut throats
Lay beside
A mug of steaming tea."
    Killkof thought a moment
Then declared,
"Poetry lies
In the heart that beats
Under the nylon smock."

5

I have come to this place,
Solitary, except for
Sheep and grouse,
For words have to be said.
    Here, beyond the Cow and Calf
Among the heather and bilberry
In this desolate spot
Secrets may be mentioned.
    Here, where Bradford
Hangs a dirty cloud

On the horizon
I may shout and stammer
Throw my arms about.
    You are no Gentle Jesus
Lover of little children
Babes die at their
Mothers' empty dugs,
Do you hear their cry
Merciful God?
    There is a man I know
Who shall be nameless
In whom a devil lives.
This man,
Who shall remain anonymous,
Has lost his mind.
He walks the streets
Speaking to the people
Words without a
Social discontent.
In short, this man
Whose signature remains a secret
Is mad
And he contends that God
Is mad also.
    Predator,
Loitering the sky
On quiet wings
Zoom in on me.
Fell me.
With vicious beak
Tear out these
Ingrown eyes.
Cleanse the bone
Of flesh.
Let the wind
Browse or rage
In my rib cage,
Skull become
A playground for
The worm, bracken

Frond erupting
Through my pelvis.

6

What Mr Snodgrass said
Was never clever
But very loud,
As though he could
Convince himself
By volume.
  He walked to
Every service on
A Sunday, sometimes
Fourteen miles for
Just one meeting;
Arriving tired and
Dusty, but ready
For a half hour
Prayer and a
Forty-minute sermon.
  Alas, it's sad to
Say, the collection for
That day was always
Down, and so was
The attendance.
  In red brick country
Chapels where tired
Farmers dozed and
Surreptitious
Nudges kept the
Shopkeepers awake,
He preached,
"The Lord is risen,"
But never could convince
Himself of this.
  Once he slid
Right down the
Pulpit rail
To show how quickly

One could fall
From Grace
Into hellfire.
Or told how in
A moment God could
Lift you from the mire.
If you liked
A good turn
Mr Snodgrass was
Your man
But there was more
Than pride behind
His well starched front.
   We, that is
My family, were
Not all that religious.
We were in fact —
Boozers. Fall in when
The door opened
Last ones out at night
Drunk as fiddlers' bitches.
Rough old scrumpy
It was too, and
A hell of a wait
Until the Monday
Prayer meeting
To whet your whistle
Again.
   There was never
Any quiet. No time
To digest what
One had listened to
The night before.
All was noise. Noise
And spittle splashing
The pulpit desk.
Shouting and madmen's gestures
As if the Kingdom
Could be won
By physical assault.

When I could walk
I was old enough!
Until I went to
Chapel I did not
Discover sin.
    First the morning school.
There I learnt about
The man up there, God,
And the bloke below
Sammy Satan. The teachers
Were too kind to speak
Ill of the devil
To little children.
    Then we all
Tramped into church
Coughing, squeaking in
Sunday boots, rustling
Sharp's toffee papers
Blowing snotty noses.
    Finally, Mr Snodgrass
Spoke.
"Now this isn't for you
Grown ups, your
Turn's later."
    Laughter from mums and dads.
"So twiddle your thumbs
Or play with a piece of string
While I talk to the bairns."
    He turned a
Ferocious eye along
The lines of lovely faces
And every private shame
Came to the surface,
It was a fair cop!
Then, to raise the
Tension he took a clean
White handkerchief
From his well-pressed
Outside pocket
And blew the walls of

Jericho to smithereens.
     O it was beautiful
To watch!
A real professional
Performance.
     All dead, all dead
     Some without a gravestone
     At their head.
After the others
Left I crept into
The family pew, where
Mum, all lavender and
Love, took me by the hand.
     And Mr Snodgrass
Black suited
Serious now
Gazed with dubiety
On the congregation.
And then confessed
When young he'd been
"A sinner,"
Just like them.
Not just
"A sinner,"
And here lay the
Poor man's sin,
The
"Biggest sinner,
Drink, never sober!
Women, all the time!
Horses, a long line of losers."
     One Saturday night
The toast being
"Round the teeth
Over the gums
Look out belly
Here it comes,"
     The Lord spoke.
"Put down that pint
Of Old and Brown,

Jeremiah Snodgrass,"
And from that day
Not a drop had
Nor had any woman
What he had lost on horses
Now fed the seven children
The Lord had blessed him with.
   Mr Snodgrass, glassy eyed
Now invited
"The drunkards
The fornicators
The racing men
To step up to
The Altar rail
Find for themselves
The mercy of His Lord."
   But no one moved
For minds were on
The mutton
Not the mercy!
   All dead, all dead
   Some without gravestone
   At their head.
Jeremiah Snodgrass
Frank Woollam
William Lamb
Arthur Atkins
James Bland
Percy English.
   A hundred names slide
Through my mind
All unknown now.
But I met Donne
And Cowper, Wesley
Watts and Newman
Bunyan, Blake,
For God was gracious
To me, though this
Thin verse scarce
Reveals my gratitude.

7

There was a man
A Park Keeper with a quiet tongue
And eyes that Hardy hoped
To be remembered for — and is.
This man was loved by no one
Yet he himself loved the loveless world
Searching with eyes like ferrets
For someone who found him lovable.
   He lived in a genteel street
Happy in a shabby room
Smelling of dust and gas.
Baked beans and other men's mean odours
Saturated his peeling walls
Like a tape recording of
The Fall from Eden.
   Every Saturday morning
Clad in his navy serge suit
Cap with a glossy peak
Black tie on light blue shirt
Regulation boots, feet purposeful
He walked to the shopping precinct
A string bag in his hand.
Boys who called
"Good morning, Parky," he noticed
With a grave nod of his head.
Boys who shouted "poxy Parky"
Were diminished by his silence.
   A person of some thirty years
Prematurely grey, his beaky nose
Accentuated his thin and grieving face.
   He was not soft, though people
Thought him simple, childlike if
You care for these distinctions.
He would for instance step
Upon the mat that worked the
Automatic doors — and then step off again!
A man so easily entertained was
Just as easily misunderstood.
He loved machinery because it showed

Lack of respect for individuals,
Or to be more precise, displayed
Small deference for the person
Suffering neither the child
Nor man of substance.
  Proud as Parky was of the
Trappings of his office, he saw
Them as a symbol of servitude.
Stand on a weighing machine
Look it straight in the pounds
Is it impressed with your lack of pence?
Place five pence in a fruit machine
And without fear or favour
Any regard for rank,
Should it feel so inclined
A pack of pastilles falls into your hand!
  Could a woman respect a man
Whose mind had never delved
Into these areas of philosophy?

8

Latch all the locks
Unleash the cringeing dogs,
The Blatant Beast
Stands on the step
Bearing gifts and malice.
  Fist knuckles the door.
The devil has my eyes
Over a burning spit,
Belly churns with hate
Boiling pitch bubbles
Inside my ears.
  "Who's there?" I cry.
"A widow from Shaw Cross
A lonely woman
Always misunderstood
Come to talk and reason,"
Replies the Blatant Beast
Wetting the tiles with tears.

91

Christ's mercy
But you can't deny
A lonely woman
Chat!
    Open the door.
She stands contained
By corsets. Dyed
And tarted up
By unskilled labour
Under a tin roof hut
Face suffused with
Choler
Voice vibrant with
Violence
False teeth
In a flaccid smile
Tits and bulging hips
Covered by plastic mac,
Thighs such as
Men dream of.
    One cannot love her,
Mutter a silent prayer,
The Blatant Beast
Has lain her axe
Against my family tree.
Straight in at the back door
Straight out through the front.
    The dogs run howling
Down the street
A cloud blocks out the sun.

9

As his desire for
Nicotine passed away
He lay in bed, half
Blind, half deaf, and
Gazed at the
Amorphous man
Who brought his food

The second child of
His loins.
   Grey as the cold ash
In his pipe he
Gave his mind to
Things that might have been.
   Mind and stomach
   Bowels and bladder
   The final solution.
He could have reached
The top. Held back by
Women, men with lesser
Talent preferred.
Sons a handicap.
Sycophants seeking power
Behind his back.
   Mind and stomach
   Bowels and bladder
   The final solution.
"I s'all have to go
To the closet, son."
The rising from the tomb
The fear along the passage.
"I s'all fall, hold
Me tight, son."
The sitting on
The pedestal.
"Are you all right, dad?"
"Ah, son, it's a mucky business!"
"Hold still while I wipe you."
"It's a mucky business!"
   Turds like tiny marbles
Leaving nothing on the paper,
The old man made as
Little mark on history.
   Stomach, bowels
   And bladder
   The final solution.

10

You can sit and
Watch the people
Passing by
Curtains drawn back
In the quiet
Of early morning.
Dog sat on your lap
No one aware
Your eyes are
Laid upon them;
Then, mid-October
Comes, and winter
Round the corner
Draws the curtain
On the scene.
"Time to get
The misses up,"
I tell the dog
And we both make
For the bedroom.
  Half way up
The stairs my mind
Is stunned, concussed
By a single word,
Charisma!
Demoralized
Knocked all
Of a heap.
Charisma!
I hurry down
Dog at heel.
There's a word
For you,
Beautiful!
  Thumbing through the
Dictionary.
Wife mumbling
"You might have
Spoken to me."

94

"It's not in
The bloody book,
A quid gone
Down the drain."
"Eat your break-
fast up," is all
She says
CHARISMA.
On the scent
Down to the Library.
I like October
It's unpredictable.
One morning and
It's mild, another
Finds a frost.
Still on the estate
Dogs peeing against
Posts, piles of paper
Lying about, old
Tins and lolly sticks,
Second rate citizens
All.
Suddenly it's
Different, the
Structures still
Resemble
Council houses
But when the
Decorating's done
The Observer not
The People
Hides the scene.
It isn't "posh",
It's private property.
By the time you reach
St Mary's,
Burglar alarms abound!
Some social workers say
That morals improve
In private dwellings.

The fallen leaves
On the park path
Are all too wet
To rustle or fly.
A solitary magpie
Sits upon a branch,
That's bad
This I was told
By mother when
A lad, but another
One flies by,
Thank God for that!
  Gardeners are
Taking up the tubers.
The earth is black,
Exciting.
A gardener rolls
A cigarette.
Another sticks his fork
Into the ground
Easing his arse
Over the handle.
They talk among
Themselves, but I pass
By without a word.
Mornings like this
And there's no need
For words.
  If it was raining
That would be quite
Different, a
"Nasty morning."
"Not a pleasant day,"
"Fair pissing it down,"
"Winter's on its way,"
Are civil greetings.
Know your man, find
The appropriate phrase
But not this morning.
  All is voluptuous.

That's a good word
Not quite right
But lovely on
The tongue,
Rich sounding.
   On the pond
Ducks all dunking
Their heads,
Lovely on water
Ungainly birds on land.
Sometimes I sit and
Watch them as they
Navigate the seas,
But not today.
   Out of the park gates
On down Catholic Hill,
That's not its proper
Name, but old folks
Call it that because
The church is there.
At the pub opposite
Joe's rattling the empties.
   I was on my seventh pint
Chatting to someone when
There's a daughter at the door
Telegram in her hand,
"Mandy's killed in car crash
Bob and Jane safe".
My eldest girl's child
Just a fortnight old.
Dead!
You can't get at Him
As He broods
Among His children.
He moves his pawns
And watches the reaction.
Tears streamed down my
Face, hate bit my heart.
I don't drink there these days.
   The dual carriage

Way was thick
With foul smelling
Diesel fumes.
I tried to find a
Gap between the lorries
Before breathing,
But a man could
Die that way
Suffocate before
He could inhale.
    Approaching the library now.
In a sweat. Sometimes
I think I'll topple
Over the edge
Of my control,
Past toleration point.
    Pulling the Oxford
Dictionary out
Palms clammy
Legs shaking
I take it to
A table.
    I'd got there,
It's an achievement,
The keeping going
To the end of day.
    But what had I gone for?
The word had vanished
From my mind like
Birdsong from the world.
O that beautiful word,
That delectable word,
    What has the
    Beginning done
    With my word?

11

Never go back
To Chester

Says my head,
Frightened all
Day, scared half to death
In bed.
    Down by the Dee
Fishermen
Sieve the water
With their nets.
If I walked into
The stream they'd
Make no profit
Out of me.
It's no Jordan
For seeking out
A pardon.
    Devastated
With innocence,
At thirteen
Never out of love
Held in a vice
Of guilt by
The hand of love.
    Now beside
Another river
The Calder
Life is more complicated.
I am not aware of love
Nor of being
Loved.
    I will go
To the waters
Of my river.
Of its slime
And putrid smell
My blubbermouth
Shall drink.
Self-deceit and
Pride will not
Defile its flow.
I will take

My sores to
The open sewer
Of hope,
Christ has been known
To search for
Sinners there,
For His Mother's sake.

Mrs Grabowski

Mrs Grabowski
Thirty years out of Poland
Short, fat out of her mind
Head stockful of flowers.
In a clean council house
Duster in distraught hand
Looking for things to distract her.
Her husband, given pride of place
On the living-room sideboard,
Looked out with gin-sodden eyes
At the woman he'd destroyed.
  Beneath the frame
And all around the house
Lilac and azaleas,
Scent and colour of spring flowers
Bludgeoned the senses
Into a daze of sweet delight.
  Mrs Grabowski
Fingers picking the dead and wilting
Out of jam jar and vase
Tongue clucking
Reproached herself
For the neglected shrine.
Loneliness
Lack of desire to speak
Had atrophied her
Vocal chords.

It was enough to be
Lost in a world of silence
That freed her from abuse.
Shopping was procured with
Pointed finger and mime
Thought had vanished from her faculties.
  Mrs Grabowski
Lived
An animal
All instinct.
  People were nice
And she would smile
Ducking her head
Or nasty
Then she scurried by
Eyes on the pavement
Head dizzy with
Uncomprehended fears.
  Clucking her tongue
Arms filled with faded flowers
Refusing to see the ultimate
She pushed them into the dustbin.
  Sometimes she cried,
A low animal noise
At the destruction of
The once so beautiful.
But today, sun shining
From cloud speckled sky
Wind warm, birds bursting
With their mating song
She picked up her wicker basket
And set out for the park.
  Mrs Grabowski
Surrounded by
Shrubs and trees
Foraging birds
Butterflies and bees
Heavy with nectar
Sought only the broken blossom
The trodden on bloom.

No perfect flower
Entered her basket
They remained, blessed
By her holy eyes.
  Happy at last
Her scarf thrown
Over her flowers
She tottered home
On shoes worn down
At heel, stockings
Around her ankles
Hair amuck
Beautiful in a world
Of selfish men.

Out of Season
For C and M

I will sit in
The shade of this
Willow and watch
The water meander
Its thoughtless course
Past Dewsbury.
  It means little
To me, who was
Baptised by an
Unknown man over
The kitchen sink
At Swaffham.
  Perhaps I cried
As I do now
The tears running
In rivulets through
The bearded mass
On my cheeks.
For a Man looked

For fruit in my heart
And nothing there
Could feed His appetite
So He cursed me
And went about
His business.
    Do not ask me
The way, stranger
I have been lost
For longer than I knew.
    One could almost
Reach out one's hand
And stroke the sky.
Move a cloud around
With a twisted finger.

I Am

    I am
Grown old before my time
Heel and hand
Cold in summer
Body broken
Skull still cupping
A youthful mind.
    I
Stretched out
A crucifix
Nailed to the earth
By the iron eye
Of God.
He hid His
Face from me
For reasons that
I understand.

Was there love in this?
I shall die
In a Dewsbury dawn
The wind off the
Snowbound Pennines
Roaring through Crow Nest Park.

Desperation

Moving in desperation
Punching my shape through air
Moving by marking time.
  The kingdom sees violence
  A flowering of forget-me-nots
  A hedge of singing birds.
God of water and stone
All inanimate things
Beside the Jordan
Wind blows through my blood.
  God of all and the particular
  Beside the Calder
  Wind chills my marrow.
God of old men
The morning star
Hurricane and whisper
Speak louder, open my eyes.
  God of the desert
  Though I stand on barren land
  Tears running down my face
  Bring out the tiny flowers.
Permit me to remain by water.

Poem

The young women
Do not wear flowers
In their hair
During the spring
And summer
Solstices
    But all year round
They spit
        With great precision

The Tied Cottager
Langham

Where I was
Dishonest
Enough to think
I was
Honest, and
Took exception
To Murry's
Mistress!
Bursting with
Plowman's lunches,
Midnight readings
Of Rabelais,
Rebelling against
A non-existent
Authority,
Wishing to be
Freed from freedom
Told what to do,
Respecting no one.
Ill, I went
Home, and a
Doctor gave me

105

Pills and sympathy.
Though I left
A time, I never
Lost the need
To return.
Brief spells near
Stratford-on-Avon
And fair Brigg
Hardly distracted
Me. People were
Dying all around
I didn't
Feel involved
With war or
People. Jesus,
I stunk the
World out with
My pride, almost
I saw myself
A Saviour!
Embraced in
Candy floss, I'll
Not burst through
This curtain, nor
Find comfort
In the social
Strata. A
Million monkeys
Typing for a year
Could not express
My loss, and yet,
I wasn't sure
What I had lost,
Never being aware
Of possessing
Anything.
    Bach's Matthew Passion;
What a
Threadbare story
To pass down

The centuries
Into the garden
Of this house
In Essex!
That cold, bright
Easter Sunday
We sat, not
Christians, pious
Men, interested
In the Arts.
Eager to show
Our virtues
To passing villagers,
Eccentrically
Dressed, immodestly
Hirsute. The
Tragedy ran its
Course. We switched
Off and went
To tea; where
I sat opposite
My wife, but
Was completely
Unaware this
Was to be.
But recognition
Came, and eager
To be desperate
I pursued her.
Through the "big
house" to Little
Oaks, into the
Shepherd and Dog,
Down to Bensusan's
Wood where I
Felled her with
A platter of
Beethoven's Seventh
Conducted by
Toscanini.

Never was man
So touched in all
His parts with
Love as I.
While Ann, bemused
And married to
Another man, though
Holding my thanks
Offering in her
Belly, hated the
Known, and feared
The unknown too,
Walking with
Vacant face the
Lovely world.
We moved a
Mile or so
Away, and were
Refused the horse
For transportation,
On moral grounds!
A run down
Cottage on the Ipswich Road
Was our first
Home. Settled in
A hollow which
Army lorries roared
Into, changed gear
And then charged
On. There were
Nightingales; a
Bucket in a
Crazy wooden hut.
Bullaces, a
Bitter plum for
Our dessert.
We were not
Very happy, but
Thrashed our bodies
Into a submission

That made us
Necessary to
Each other.
It was untidy
Living. Guilt
Gave us apple
Pie beds, sex
Dulled our senses.
Grief reached the
Pole Star and
Beyond, we soon
Lost our direction
Walking this
World with
Vague hope in
A nearly unknown
God.
November came
And set us
Off for London,
But what went
On there isn't
Worth repeating.
We waited for
A birth, and
Were not dis-
Appointed.

Bottom Barn

January, sun
Down on its knees
In morning prayer.
The first house for
My family, furniture
Scattered around. Love
In a frenzy on
The bare wood floor
Reborn in bedroom
When harvest homed

And pheasants strut
The stubble.
A house a half
A mile from the
Bath Road. Reached
By a rutted track
Ending at the
Gateway to a
Meadow. Only the
Royal Mail comes
To our door, others
Leave parcels at
The end of lane
Where thieves steal
Milk and bread.
In front, a brick
Built barn, mangers,
Covered yard, where
Bullocks snort among
The straw.
If I forget you
Bottom Barn
Let my mind
Find peace in
This sad world.
Beyond the barn
Two fields, a
Hundred acres each
Where in the summer
Paratroopers
Fall, and I
Find silk to clothe
My first child with,
White for the
Innocence we both
Look back on.
Behind, a wooden
Hut for our
Convenience.
An iron pump

Outside the door
Whips water all
Direction when
The wind blows
From the West.
And no more
Concessions
To our comfort.
Then, a long
Thin field,
Permanent pasture
Unploughed in
The memory of
The oldest man.
Here in the spring
An acre of wild
Violets; mullein
And pink mallow
In profusion.
Evening
A red hot heifer
Thunders past the
House. Mice take
My peas. The owl
That lays her eggs
Upon the ledges
Of the barn
Pierces the silence.
Beyond the meadow
A hanging of
Beech shelters
Us from the East,
And keeps our
Fender warm.
No neighbours to
Fall foul of.
Sometimes a week
Went by 'til Jacko
Brought my wages
And walked the

Young wheat with
Me as I searched
For docks. A quiet
Man who told in
Minutes what
Occurred in days.
In this small
Depression
Three years running
Frost blacked my
First potatoes
And I cried
A curse upon
The weather!
Greens turning
Steely blue for
Want of rain,
Impotent I stood
Watching each
Passing cloud
With earthborn eyes,
Until among the
Men I damned
The sky, and
Forecast drought
Whenever they
Saw messengers
In the West.
A month crawled
By before a tiny
Shower damped the
Leaves, and I
Won respect.
March once found
Me harrowing with
Three horses, the
Hares so tame
They clowned about
The clods I tried to break.
Tractor drivers

Circled them
Indian fashion
Until the hares
In trance were
Clubbed with
Plough paddles.
At first I
Was affected
By the sight.
Mornings: stood
On the oily
Earth of the
Tractor shed,
Forced by habit
To be ten
Minutes early.
Frightened by
The entrance of
The other men,
Making placatory
Remarks, easing
The morning's
Animosity
Over my shivering
Shoulders.
As we approached
The wheat rick,
A stoat in winter
White fled from
Its sheltering thatch.
The rats burrowed
Down into the
Bedding as we,
Old Freddy Brown
And me, pitched
Layer after
Layer of sheaves.
The day so still
Clack of the
Driving belt

Sounds like
A bull whip.
"Mason" feeding
In the sheaves
Swearing at
The driver.
Above the board
Pitching was easy
Allowing time to
View the sky
And bordering
Hedges where birds
Went about their
Business.
But as we
Progressed down
The rick, the
Dust and chaff
Fell on our
Faces. Eyes began
To water, nose
To run: arms
Tired, one no
longer noticed
Clouds or birds
Being reduced
To aching muscles
And a throat.
Sod a job that
Always seems
To hand you out
The worst. Eye
Envied the chaff
Gatherer, stub
In his gossiping
Mouth, the sackman,
Any man not tied
To this wretched
Rick.
At bedding level

Jack Russells
Scamper behind
Wire netting
Set up around
The base. Rats
Make me think
That there's some
Hope for man.
The morning beaver
A gulp of tea
A bite of bread
And cheese. Then
A Woodbine.
"I see'd old
Pitman up the
Road a hare hung
From his shoulder."
Faces make no
Move. Onion
Is sliced.
"He ain't no right
To that for
That be game" says
Old Tom Pike.
Scratching of heads
And matches.
Delicately
Someone says,
"Best not the
*Hon*ourable catch
Him at it,"
And back to
Pitching sheaves.
If there was
Nobility it
Was not visible
Though stoicism
And courage,
Animal survival
Could be seen.

And just because
Their plight was
Mine I found
That I could
Love them.
Spring caught us
With our Home
Guard coats on,
Winter without
Our woolly pants.
The seasons turned
Their backs on
What the clock
Said, and government
Decree passed by
Unnoticed.
Farmers were bribed
To plough and
Plant potatoes,
A scandal that
Seemed to pass
Unrecognized.
We entered my
Eldest child in
The Kintbury baby
Show, and were
Surprised she
Didn't win.
September heard
The birth cry
Of my second.
After the cleaning
Up I was allowed
To see her; held
High in the mid-wife's
Hands, an offering
To the Gods.
Who threw the
Black despair
Over our roof,

Set your face
In cement, no
Joy in sight?

Sherborne

A mistake
Right from the
Start.
Two different
Men and one
Reply
Found me in
The wrong place
With the wrong
Man
Who not expecting
Me, when I
Turned up
Gave me the
Job!
The other
Waited for
The luncheon
Bell,
Then took his
Gun into the
Woods and blew
Holes in his
Head.
   There was beauty,
Yes, but I
Never could shout
God out of
The sky.
Those gloomy strides
Over the trout
Strewn stream
Ulcers and
Abscesses

In painful
Places.
Cows with the
Husk.
Man with a
Scented hand-
Kerchief, and
Nothing else
To speak of.
    A King died
And the bagpipes
Played "The Flowers
Of the Forest".
Gamekeeper shot
The cat!
Departure in
A cattle truck
Foolish enough
To hope for
Better things.

Paulerspury

And my largest
Herd, procured
By bribery!
"You can have the
Job if your
Kids attend
The Sunday School."
"Done" I said
Desperate for
A home, and then
Was shown a
Council house,
All mod-cons.
With it I saw
The chance to gain
Release from the
Tied Cottage. All was

Agreed, but when
The cattle truck
Arrived at Paulerspury
We were shown an
Old red house with
Water pump outside,
A roof that let
In rain, window
Frames that fell
In when the wind
Blustered.
Not the council
House we had
Been promised!
I bawled and
Blustered — all to
No avail. Once
More I had
Been done, this
Time by a
High pitched voice
And non-conformist
Cunning. The
Children, tired
Hungry, knickers
Wet, were led
Inside; the fire
Lit, furniture
Set about the
House. The lorry
Left a crying
Woman and a
Vicious man.
Once more we
Had to mind
Our tongues, smile
At trifles, please
The boss or find
Ourselves without
A roof over

Our heads.
If tears had
Been tidal waves
Curses thunderbolts,
The farm would
Have laid in ruins.
The cows, the
Biggest herd of
Jerseys then in
Britain, assuaged
My battered pride,
But I never
Trusted the shifty
Face that gazed at
Feet and left
My eyes to
Wander on his
Vanity.
One side the
Watling Street
Menaced our dreams,
To cross that
Road needs courage.
Madmen and
Motorcyclists pointing
For Silverstone,
Or punters set for
Towcester, just
As dangerous.
Ginny frightened
Us with death
Lying one night
In crisis. We
Listened to her
Sick lungs barking,
Afraid to sleep
Lest death should
Catch us unawares.
The fever fell,
She slept.

I pulled the
Sheets around
Her shoulders,
God grateful.
   My brother
Man with stretch
Nylon morals
Pounded our door
And ears with
Tales of turpitude.
Father giving
Seventy a thump
Had lost his
Heart to some
Sad wife deserted
For the gin.
"Let us" said he
Churchillian in
Style, "Let us
Face the sinner."
What nonsense,
And what
Effrontery!
Father had an
Eye for pretty
Women, a romantic
Who never laid
A lover, nor
Had the courage.
If I had
Felt less fear
For the good
Man, I could
Have loved him
More. Too late,
Too late, he
Is cared for by the re-
spectable son.
His weeds concealed
By marble stone,

Flowers, not mine
Above his head.
In time he
Will become
A gentleman!
May I record
He slept in his
Vest, pants, and
Socks, and seldom
Took a bath.
Lost his ambition
At an early
Age, did little
Or nothing but
Hang on till
His end.
  Down by the
Stream there stood
A tree, as
Sweet a tree
As you could
See. Crab apple,
Blaze of blossom
In spring, ingots
Of bronze in
Autumn.
I have stood
And watched this
Tree, full of
Dreams, thinking
If fate had
Only given me
A glance, or
God a blessing,
The irritant of
Art could have
Been scratched,
The itch relieved.
In shitty gumboots
Straw strewn hair

I asked for
What at that
Time I considered
Were my dues;
It never entered
My mind I was
Receiving them.
Cows died of
Bloat, I used
The trocar on
My wife. One
Wet November
Morning, unable
To stand, I
Crawled through
Dung and mud
Calling the cows
In, and then
Crawled home to
Lie in bed
Four weeks,
Unaware it
Was the beginning.
    A foolish man,
A traveller —
Not fellow —
Took to visiting
Me. I, being
Foolish also,
Recognized the fellow.
Left the con-
stipation of
Non-conformity
For Harpenden,
And the in-
continence
Of an idiot's
Temper. Drifting
With the purpose
Of a matchstick

123

In a guttered
Stream. There I
Am, look, going
Down the drain,
Again!

Harpenden

One year there
Reduced me to
A shivering wreck.
I have no
Appetite for
Anger, no
Stomach for
A scene. This
Redfaced bully
Fat, illmannered
A tyrant to
The ageing lady
Of the house,
Installed me
In her property
Then pulled it
Down on me.
Perpetual fear
Robbed me of
Will and wit.
I would wait for
His wrath to
Explode,
Anticipating
Every choleric
Outburst a
Hundred times.
I thought of
Dying on the
Nearby railway
Line. Stood on
The bridge, beaten

By a fool.
My mind centred
On this man,
Fears festered
Until I found
It difficult
To find my
Voice when in
His company.
"Where is the
Milk? She gave
Nineteen pounds
Yesterday, today
Only eighteen,
Where is the
Milk?" Too daft
To answer is
The ignorance
Of the stupid.
After a year
I gave my
Notice in although
I had no job
To go to.
Ann in a
Nervous breakdown,
Weeks cartwheeling
Into months and
All confused in
Dreams, sat out
The battle in
Appalling
Silence. We
Were chastised
For our trans-
gressions, God
Hid His face
Among the stars
And left us
In a dark

Place. We prayed
The bailiffs might
Not put us
On the street,
A man near
Shenley heard.

High Canons

For a time
I did well
At High Canons.
The farmer liked
To spend his
Days at market
Leaving me in
Control. A
"How's things, Cliff"
At evening,
And that was
All I saw
Of him. A
Heifer held
Her calf so
Tight, seven
Men couldn't
Move it! I
Tried to haul
It out by
Tractor, no good.
I rang the vet
Who cut the calf
To pieces in
Its mother. I
Was matter
Of fact about
Such things, calm
In a crisis,
But family
Life was drooping

126

Like unwatered
Succulents.
I fell out
And into
Love with one
Who was too
Young for me.
Never did
Spring and bird
Song sound like
This. My feet
Moved over plough
Land with a
Dancer's joy, but
In my heart
I knew that she
Was living in
Archer land.
Ann took herself
To hospital
For three months.
The sun shone
As we mounted
Napsbury steps
Where Sister
Gave me back
The scissors
We had packed
Saying such things
Were "not required
There." I was
Too innocent or
Too daft to
Understand just
Why. Twice a
Week I cycled
Shenley Hill,
A nasty brute,
Trying to
Be a husband

And a father
One was proud of.
I even found
A face to
Keep the farmer
Happy. But worry
Bit into my
Heart and muscles,
Made me forget
Just who I was.
Returning to
The dairy every
Night to make
Sure I had
Turned the water
Off, something
I knew I'd
Done, but dare
Not take for
Granted. Ann
Came back home
Knowing she hated
Her father, whom
She had for
Years, but needed
Re-assurance,
The approval
Of society
To ease her guilt.
The final harvest
Found me quite
Unable to pitch
A bale of straw.
Once more I
Took to bed
Back broken
And heard the
Doctor say, "You've
Had enough, Cliff,"
Forbidding me

To milk a cow
Again. I lay
Head pinned to
Pillow, farmer's
Son stood at
My side, cards
In his hand,
Court order
Promised for the
House. It came
As no surprise.
The soil asserts
Authority,
Ploughs ephemeral
Flesh into the
Ground, breaks the
Strongest will,
Claiming what
It first moulded.

The Hill

At the bottom of the hill
A sign, advertising a cheese
Factory closed five years ago.
Half way up, as one would expect
The medical practitioners
Attend to sickness by appointment.
The church that straddles the road
On top the hill conducts
Its business in a similar fashion.
But the red-brick weathered wall
Lining the right hand side
Really makes one marvel.
In the interstices, where time has
Crumbled the mortar to a softer
Substance, beautiful, delicate weeds

Make root and hold against
The winter's whine.
They live because they are there
And where they are life can find
A finger hold. Those who walk by
Try to find some reason for existence.
    Stand at the bottom of the hill
In the right place, and church bells
Crash out from the wrong direction.

Poem

Laid in my lap
Whose is that old man's hand?
Is that one of my children?
What is this taste upon my tongue
Tintinnabulation in my ear?
    Four Angels stand at points about my bed
    Where He is closer to me than my neighbour.

O the ache of being what I seem.

Dewsbury

Incite me to love
This shoddy town
And its inhabitants
Who, surrounded by their
"Special Offer" homes
Dream of a city
Where there is no night.
Where there is no night

The darkness never
Penetrating its golden walls,
Everlasting birdsong floating
In the splendid air.

I Would Not Ask

I would not ask
For I would not expect
The Son of God
To live within the confines
Of these shabby clothes.
Nor that His love would stray
Into the clapped out
Ventricles of this heart
And flower in my blood
As love.

  Wind whips down the river
  I feel the pulsing in my ribs
  Night finds me unprepared.

Naked

The sun catches the pink
Of the azaleas.
All through the winter
Heart as black as pitch
I have groped within my box of pills
Searching for salvation —
The bowels of Christ denied me this.
Young man I laid upon the ground,

If God saw violence then I would be violent,
Beating the stones with bruised and bloody fists
But the Keeper of the Gate remained unmoved.
  I rose up from the earth strangely chastened.

With Roughened Sighs

With roughened sighs
The East Wind snores and snuffles
Through the ginnel.
From Bob's Emporium
The smell of frying fish
Batters my person.
A bicycle tyre hangs
From a lamp post
Bowed in silent prayer.
Night, the frost nibbles
At the hem of my distress.

Unpopular Opinions

Delicate Dale and cosy Cookson
Print their arty, bow-tied stuff
And the poems in PNR?
One cannot say they're up to snuff!
Something's vanished from the language
Once so vigorous and grand
And what's left is pap and pobbies
Neatly writ — but very bland.
John Skelton once gave birth to words
Undisciplined but full of power
As though they were being coined and cast
To legal currency by the hour.
And Anon like an honest man

Declined to pretty up and say
What happened to A Serving Girl
Upon Her Holiday.
Indeed it never would occur
To boil the good red meat to jelly
But tell the tale of chest to tit
And cock to cunt and belly to belly.
At later date poor mad mild Clare
Put sweeter songs in a thrushes throat
But Hardy, Barnes and Edward Thomas
Left thin grey tack in the gravy boat.
Well to be fair the times had changed
They couldn't say again
What had been said by better poets —
But they were gentlemen
And no one would deny or try
To doubt their capability
But what comes out is mainly
A middle-class sensibility.

Latter Day Psalm

Search out my blemishes, Lord
Investigate these bones,
For my head is full of shadows
And through the channels of my blood
Fear runs amuck.
When I would speak with you
What dribbles from my tongue
Are stale requests.
   Insinuate the crevices of my mind
Remove the evil vestments from my heart
For my eyes cannot see God
My ears dull to His word
There is no pleasure in my children.

A View

1

I have sat watching
Many Sunday nights
Ecstasy on the face
Of well-dressed women
Singing the Sabbath hymns.

Or

Noticed while walking
Hopton Woods
The sexuality of trees.
Seen sallow sun
Emerge from winter sky
And light a spirit
That had dropped to earth.

2

This man
Turning into himself
Found
A stranger with
A cloven hoof.
That man
Exploring in
An uncaring world
Drowned
In his own distractions.

Poem

My voice has lost its Frank Sinatra feeling
My trumpet imitations now sound flat,
I have no moral feelings about stealing
I eat and drink less yet I still grow fat.

The love I once gave gladly to my brother
I find now hardly stretches to my dog,
I don't suppose we really like each other
There's not enough affection left to log.
Too man "I's" too many "my's" so selfish
They punctuate the rhythm pride has played,
My outer surfaces rival the shellfish
Hate lingers, O — I wish that love had stayed.

An Exercise in Trivia

The cabbage whites that flutter
Round the washing on this
Limp June day, seem as uncertain
Where to go as I am doubtful
What to say. The woman striding
Down the path, "O" levels finished
Yesterday, has hung her blazer
Up for good and gone to work at
Lesstopay. These observations
May not please the poets discussing
Overly — they haven't got a
Lot of wit — life's ecstasy and
Agony. May I just say in
Manner mild, that on this point I
Do agree, but one has got to
Pass the time between the morning
Meal and tea. Of course I could have
Clipped the hedge, in fact I tried and
Hurt my back, oh what a beautiful
Excuse to wander down and
See the quack. The other week I
Noticed that he'd bought a spanking new
Mercedes, purchased by seeing
Nuts like me, and reassuring preg-
Nant ladies. Last time I saw him

He remarked, "You seem a lit-
Tle thinner," I would write more but
Ann has knocked to say it's time
For dinner.

A Tribute
for C.H. Sisson's Seventieth Birthday

His real ambition was
To nurture things, not people
Though he did this too.
Like the grave his heart
Is a private place where emotion
Is deliberately kept at a low temperature.
So writing verse fulfilled, to some degree
His farming instincts.
I have watched him
In his garden turning soil
And wondered what flowering
Might emerge from this
Well tendered tilth.
A poet of the overlooked
His poems resound with bells
Sun scented blooms
Small shells and birdsong.
Even the empty air
Is filled with wonder
As he milks the muse
With tender dedication.

Poem

Poor young girl
Poor young girl
Caught on the horn
Of a young man's dilemma
Poor young girl.

Poem

"Look!" She raised an arm
Pointing into the distant hills,
And her dress fell round her body
In lines that disturbed my crutch.
There being no one in sight,
The evening late, I placed
A hand over her breasts and we collapsed
An untidy tangle in the bracken.

Dreaming

I would have been
Happy to be the man
Leaning against the wall
As Fred Astaire danced,
Cameras in attendance,
Down Park Avenue.
Or a chorus boy,
Some poor hoofer
Full frontal grin in view,
Filling the back row
In a Dick Powell movie.
It would have been an honour
To be knocked down

By Gary Cooper's horse
As it loped through arid
Western towns pursuing villainy,
Coop, — tall in the saddle.
Yup.
Or waiting table
In Fortysecond Street,
Serve Lester Young a shot of rye
And listen to Roy Eldridge
Blowing *Hecklers Hop*.

But destiny had other plans for me.
At fourteen a fashion shop
In Boar Lane, Leeds,
Dressed in striped trousers:
Monkey jacket and white shirt:
Hair in subjection to Macassar oil.
One who jumped
At the shop assistant's cry,
"Windows, Mr Ashby!"
Star-eyed and dreaming my youth away
Pleating diamante-covered evening gowns.

Poem

"Ah"
The man I thought
That I would be,
"Oh"
The man I am.

Two Old Men

His bedroom smells
Of dirty clothes and
Piddled-in pants.
As one eats breakfast
The chamber pot
Is poured into
The porcelain before
His first appearance.
It's a desperate
Situation. One
Sees oneself a
Few short years ahead,
Incontinent,
Staggering from
Chair to chair.
Respected for
One's length of
Days and depth
Of pocket.
I hate him
And he knows.
To hide the fact
A bottle of gin
Lies beside my bed
He keeps the
Stereo on loud.
Half pissed, half
Deafened I try
To be a credit
To his daughter.

Blackbird

Blackbird, singing in
The wet, bare branches
Of my tree,
Take your song
And when the sun
Issues its challenge
To the day,
Tell the good folk
Of Heckmondwike
That I too am aware
Life might have been
Other than it is.

Poem

It's hard to put the words down —
Not the physical effort,
But the demand for truth
Makes every word suspect.
So poetry is lies and half-truths
A reflection of us all,
Though I can only speak for myself.

A Tragic Tale

And he would have told her
Of his love
In the dog days of summer
Briar roses clambering
Up the hawthorn
The Nidd strolling quietly
Down to Knaresborough.
He, foot clumsy collar tight
Filled with prayer meeting passion

Would have told her
Of his love.
But she
All proud and delicate
Made conversation with
Her eldest sister,
Ignored the timid youth
Who trailed behind
Except when swooping on
A buttercup or Soldiers Button
Crying with ecstasy at
Some fish leaping for a fly.
    And so they came to Bilton
Mumbling inexperienced goodbyes,
Saying they might meet at
Morning service, Dragon Parade.
Then they went home.
She to cold potatoes and cold meat
A mother's relentless eye
He to scones spread thick
With oven-cooked bacon.
Mouth full but unreproached —
For was he not the youngest
And were not his bad manners
Forgiven before committed —
He blurted out
"I've met the girl that I intend to marry."
Of course they were delighted
And amused.
"Bless the boy" said grandma,
A sister,
"Our Harold is a card!"
Be that as it may
There was a wedding day
And an Ashby was united
With a King.
    They lived their loveless days
    One driven by vanity
    The other pursued by fear.
    Both died with little hope.

141

Dog Hill

Come on, bitch
Let's up Dog Hill
The unemployed
Exercising
The unemployable.
Above the spewing Spen
A depression of estates
Spreads over each aspiring hill,
Fields of hope diminish
The tree of joy is felled.

At Merriscourt in harvest weather
A fox, in a feathered reverie
Strolled through my herd of cows.
The evening sun caught
Shipton under Wychwood,
All my children were asleep
And love seemed not a lie.

She sympathized —
"At sixtyfour
You can't do more
Than what you did
Around a score."
And I knew that I was old.

One two three
Magpies in a tree
What's to become of me?

Easter Skipping Song
For Sonali

Christ is up with a hobbledeho
Tripmalarityganzy
Six of His salesmen stood in a row
Tripmalarityganzy
A spinster opens the door a crack
Tripmalarityganzy
Two kestrels mate on the chimney stack
Tripmalarityganzy
The sun comes out with a "view halloo"
Tripmalarityganzy
The seagulls howl and the dogs all mew
Tripmalarityganzy
When I am old I'll sit in a chair
Tripmalarityganzy
My grandaughters two will wash my hair
Tripmalarityganzy
With water drawn from the crystal Spen
Tripmalarity ganzy
Pig in a palace pope in a pen
Tripmalarityganzy.

Hindsight

When sight was sound
And every sound was relayed
To the senses, life seemed endless
And each moment missing from
The loved one an eternity.
But now my darling reading
The obituaries it seems, friends
Fade like flowers and every face
One confronts in the street
May look familiar but must be
Dead or different.

143

Where is that goal of peace
That we pursued?
Now eyes strain, ears are on the wane
The aches and pain of age
Rock us as with calloused feet
We stumble towards anonymity.

I Start

I do nothing
Earlier than I did
A year ago,
I need a longer day
To get my worrying done.
Under occupied,
Over indulged,
When the gin starts to work
Stand by your telephones, friends,
Ashby is on the prowl asking for love.
 It's doubtful if you'll
   Get a hint of his.

The Fisherman's Daughter
Peel

I would walk down Derby Road
Holding my love a secret,
Eyes on my clumsy boots in fear
Someone should see into my heart.
Or laid in bed conjure up her face;
Brown eyes that spoke to me alone,
Or so I thought:
Black hair I dare not touch —
Not even in a dream.

Should we pass along the harbour wall
Or in school corridor, so weak my legs
I thought that I would faint.
A curse upon my non-conformist nose
Offended by the smell of her father's trade.

War Poem

Her face was calm
Her body had the lines of grace.
"Who" I asked, "is that gentlewoman
Riding so often into Kintbury?"

She had five children.
Two by her husband
One in a union with some U.S. serviceman
Two more by her father.
He, when learning of her intended marriage
Took her and shotgun into a distant field
Blasted one barrel in her face
Then blew himself away.
She lived face scarred
Vanishing into London
A week or more at a time
With some lost soul from Arkansas
Or Tallahassee.
Always returning to tend her young
She faced the hamlet with indifferent pride.

A more incestuous clutter of cottages
The killing soil never revealed to me,
But I was happy there
Made aware of my true depravity.
Surrounded by men who never found toil
A panacea for living
Unable to differentiate between the two.

Poem

I am too much
Like a man
I do not admire.
Quick to anger
Speaking ill
Of everyone
Satisfied with nothing
Loving nobody.
　　Look! the lilac has come out.

Heckmondwike Poem

There is a confusion
In my head. A madness
As chaotic as the universe
Before the mind of God
Brought order to the stars
And put each living creature
In its proper place.
There is a confusion
In my heart where love
Longing to spread about
The objects that my eye perceives
Remains locked in the prison
Of my sad timidity.
Another May — the rhododendrons weep.
Love hardens in the young
And age attempts again
To square its shoulders.
Winter has passed
But spring can still
Do violence to the old.

On Seeing Hall Caine
Peel — I.O.M. — 1920s

He was standing
One foot upon
The promenade's bottom rail
Looking towards
The Mull of Galloway.
It was winter — quiet
The sea so still
Sky bluer than now.
I think he wore a cloak
A funny hat, a beard,
Certainly he was different
Displaying an absorption
That confounded me.

Everything so still
And I so young.

Perhaps I imagined this
Or heard someone describe the scene?
It is vague —
As are my memories
Of being a child.
Was I ever younger
Than I am now?

Friends

When you reach old age
Don't try to find lost friends.
It seems the best are dead
Those left not as remembered
While some shout through the keyhole
"Go away".

147

I search among the people in the street
For unlined faces
Such as I imagine mine to be
And meet old age, stooped shoulders
Generous figures and ungenerous minds.
It seems that friendship
Starts with admiration,
Grows into a comfortable habit,
Then desiccates and dies.
Those I once loved
I find I now despise.

Not Every Seed

Not every seed that's sown turns out to be
Fit for the show bench or a fruitful tree.
Some fall on stony ground in time of drought
Some germinate and put their seed leaves out
But fall a victim to the slug or fly
The pigeons' crop or heel of passerby.
And so with men, who in God's image made,
End up behind a desk or in some trade
Chosen by parents as a last resort
For dreaming children with a poor report.
Not to be clever is a fine disguise
For those who seek the wisdom of the wise
And turn their faces from the sickening mess
Of those who seek the wisdom of success.

Green Peace

"When morning gilds the sky"
It's time to gather up
One's fears and drown them
In a pint of Doctor Green.

Someone has said, I've seen
It in a book, "The unknown
Is what man is frightened of".
But surfacing from oblivion
That has no dreams
Mouth in a conversation
The mind is ignorant of
In a place one can't remember
Getting to
Smiles of friendship
Drive one home to seek again
The comfort of a pint of Doctor Green.
Last year I missed the daphne
This the spring.
Days disappear in loneliness
The breakdown of affections
And the scaling off of talent
Until a pint of Doctor Green
Makes society's indifference bearable.

One day, perhaps, the Comforter will come
Disturbing the spirits beating Salvation's drum
Or with the wisdom plucked from a dusty shelf
Suggest somewhere I have a better self.

If fish still swam in rivers
And the old all died in bed
If pastures were unpoisoned
And the swan was free from lead
If gay was still a lovely word
And a child was safe at play
If the chicken in the battery house
Looked forward to the day
If joy still walked abroad
And man's condition was less mean
And all the dolphins were set free
What then Doctor Green?

Thoughts on a Sleepless Night

I will stand among the flowers
And let the August wind brush against my cheeks.
Night, and all the senses ask for sleep
To place a cooling hand upon the forehead.
The air so dry grit makes the eye abrasive
Seeding rosebay clutches at one's hair.
Somewhere behind me in the window box
The succulent stemmed begonias dance
In an erotic tremor.
A distant train disturbs the insomniacs' silence
Mrs Patel's child whimpers in her dream.

Dear

When we first touched
And, to use a word
That sounds old-fashioned now — kissed
Morning was music, night
Love In A Mist.
Now with glaucous eyes we glower
Resentful and unheeding,
And cruelly ignore each others needs —
Love Lies Bleeding.

152